"It's rare you find a teacher, pastor, and a[...] possesses not only the charisma of Chri[...] wisdom that is ageless. Andrew is a voic[...] influence is not self-indulgent, but truly [...] His story, like Jacob's, is one where he wrestled with God, left with a limp, and now lives boldly to testify the truth and mercy of God's glory. We should all be so blessed to glean from what God has taught him and take his practical, real-life, day-to-day prayer walk and put it into action. Favor follows obedience, and Andrew and his bride are living proof of this."

Tamra Andress, CEO and founder, F.I.T. in Faith Media
and The Founder Collective Ministry

"Next to the Scriptures, *The Privilege of Prayer* might be one of the most important books I have ever read. Andrew talks about every kind of prayer, without judgment and with encouragement, wisdom, insight, motivation, and application. This is a book I will hang on to and read again and again. I'd recommend this to anyone who wants to see God in all His glory and experience Him more personally!"

Clarence L. Smith Jr., lead pastor, Enhance Church

"*The Privilege of Prayer* is a powerful reminder of the significance of daily, consistent prayer that will empower you to take on whatever call God has on your life. Andrew masterfully shares the truth in love through his use of Scripture and personal experiences with the power of being in the presence of God. No matter what your place in ministry is, this book will remind you of God's invitation to spend time with Him each day, and His amazing purpose for your life."

Caleb Rouse, relationship counselor; digital creator; author

"In his compelling book *The Privilege of Prayer*, Andrew presents a fresh and powerful perspective on the privilege of talking with our Creator. Andrew's story is real, raw, and authentic. This insightful read is perfect for those who are new to their faith journey and are seeking a deeper understanding of prayer, as well as for anyone looking to reignite their prayer life. I highly recommend this insightful book!"

Ramzi Fakhoury, writer and creator, Coffee With My Father

"Prayer is like spiritual breathing in a world that is suffocating for lack of spiritual oxygen. Through practical prayer applications, Andrew's book provides this dying world with a breath of fresh air! I love this book not only because he invites you into his personal story, but because he helps lead you straight to Jesus with practical applications to grow in your prayer life!"

Craig Brown, pastor; digital missionary

"As a Christian therapist, I wholeheartedly endorse *The Privilege of Prayer*. This remarkable book captures the transformative power of prayer. Andrew's authentic storytelling and deep understanding of Scripture resonate with those seeking a more intimate connection with God. It's a profound invitation to experience His love, guidance, and purpose."

Stefanie Rouse, relationship counselor; digital creator; author

"I have known Andrew for years. He understands we cannot thrive without the depth and intimacy of prayer that he describes in a beautifully simplistic way. Andrew speaks on prayer not as someone who has it all figured out, but rather as someone who's on the journey. *The Privilege of Prayer* is refreshing, convicting, and insightful. This book on prayer will be an answer to prayer for many. Grab several copies and gift them!"

Rashawn Copeland, co-founder, Share The King;
author, *Start Where You Are*

"This is the prayer book you've been waiting for! Whether you're a seasoned prayer warrior or new in your journey, you will have many aha moments. Andrew's time in the secret place has made him a deep well. I can read this book repeatedly and still receive insight. So good!"

Roxanne Grace, DREAM Label Group; host, *The Conversation*
podcast; host at KWAVE 107.9

"Andrew Carter is the real deal. He shows up consistently to his worldwide audience and is an even better friend to me and many others. He takes prayer seriously and invites people to experience the power of implementing prayer into the rhythm of their lives and how it has the power to change lives."

Joshua Broome, co-founder, Share The King; author

"When you begin to understand what prayer means, you will begin to realize the privilege of prayer. In this book, Andrew Carter takes us along the pathway of prayer on a journey of discovery. There is no question that this book will help you gain a deeper understanding of prayer than you have ever had before."

Marcus Stanley, co-founder, Onewayhope

THE
PRIVILEGE
OF
PRAYER

THE PRIVILEGE OF PRAYER

FIND HEALING, TRANSFORMATION, AND ANSWERS

ANDREW F CARTER

Chosen
a division of Baker Publishing Group
Minneapolis, Minnesota

Published by Chosen Books
Minneapolis, Minnesota
www.chosenbooks.com

Chosen Books is a division of
Baker Publishing Group, Grand Rapids, Michigan

Printed in the United States of America

Library of Congress Cataloging-in-Publication Data
Names: Carter, Andrew Formby, author.
Title: The privilege of prayer : find healing, transformation, and answers / Andrew F. Carter.
Description: Minneapolis, Minnesota : Chosen Books, a division of Baker Publishing Group, 2023. | Includes bibliographical references.
Identifiers: LCCN 2023014041 | ISBN 9780800763510 (trade paper) | ISBN 9780800763619 (casebound) | ISBN 9781493442508 (ebook)
Subjects: LCSH: Prayer--Christianity.
Classification: LCC BV227 .C37 2023 | DDC 248.3/2--dc23/eng/20230505
LC record available at https://lccn.loc.gov/2023014041

Published in association with The Bindery Agency, www.TheBinderyAgency.com.

Baker Publishing Group publications use paper produced from sustainable forestry practices and post-consumer waste whenever possible.

23 24 25 26 27 28 29   7 6 5 4 3 2 1

This book is dedicated to those who are struggling to hear God's voice.

Contents

Introduction

Some of my earliest childhood memories are of me lying in bed talking to God. I remember laughing, crying, and having back-and-forth conversations with what adults would call an imaginary friend. Even though I didn't know much about God and who He is, I remember lying in bed asking Him random questions about what the purpose of life is, why I exist, what it meant to die, and where would I go if I died.

When I was younger, I spent many days in and out of the hospital, so questions like these piqued my interest. My mother was a prostitute, my dad was her pimp, and I'm a product of their drug affairs. My mother struggled with a drug addiction and had consumed drugs for months before she found out she was pregnant with me. As a result, I had underdeveloped lungs. I had constant loss of breath that required me to undergo breathing treatments, take lots of medication, and wrestle with severe asthma. Throughout my childhood, I fully comprehended the fact that I could take my last breath if I didn't bring my inhaler with me everywhere I went. This ultimately triggered a fear of death. Spending time in the hospital didn't help these triggers. I was surrounded by talk of the afterlife and going to Heaven when we pass away.

As years went on and I got a little bit older, I didn't just lose touch with my childhood innocence, I also lost touch with God's presence and the ability to interact with Him as I once had. With no godly counsel and guidance in my childhood, I became a very destructive teenager. I started rebelling against the adults in my life. I was a troubled kid who got attention for acting out. In my mind, receiving attention for being bad was better than not receiving attention at all.

To add to this, I grew up being mixed-race—black and white. I lived in a predominantly white state where the odds were stacked against me. I was bullied for the color of my skin and experienced racism every single day. This stirred up so many angry emotions, and I found myself getting involved with drugs, alcohol, lying, stealing, and having sex to numb the pain. This behavior carried with me into adulthood. Lost, broken, and confused, I ended up in jail multiple times.

Fast-forward to today—as an on-fire Christian and follower of Jesus, I now know that sin separates us from God. I've learned that my relationship with God must always come first and that I was created to serve Him. I've learned how to stay in alignment with God's plan and purpose for my life by staying in constant communication with Him and by understanding that prayer is a privilege. Being able to speak to God whenever, however, wherever is an absolute privilege.

I've come up with a hypothesis about childhood. Up to a certain point in our childhood, I believe we have a strong connection to our Creator even though we may not know it. We have a childlike faith that's pure and welcoming. As we embark on the journey of life and we go astray, I believe that line of communication with Him is broken. We start building walls around our heart based on life experiences. It's part of our purpose to find restoration by putting our faith in the finished work of Jesus Christ. The years between then and when we accept Jesus as our Lord and Savior are jumbled together. What seems like a blur to us is actually the road of restoring our lines of communication with God.

Communication with God is what we call prayer. That communication is only possible because of the death, burial, and resurrection of Jesus Christ. His sacrifice paid my debts by erasing it, restoring a clean slate, and giving me the ability to reconnect with God, our Father. Based on my personal journey, I'm going to share different things that have made me realize that prayer is not an option or obligation—it's a privilege. It's the essential ingredient for an effective life of following Jesus.

I will define what prayer is, show you how being consistent can improve your prayer life, give you a Scripture-based template of how we should be praying, and teach you how to navigate the answers to your prayers. God doesn't always say yes to our prayers, so we need to be prepared and ready when His answer doesn't look like what we expected. I will address the things that cause delays, resistance, and obstruction that many people face, and I will offer solutions on how to fix it.

This book will highlight the importance of following God's will and God's way; why we should repair relationships with some people; how to combat feelings and emotions; how to react to life situations like disappointments and betrayal; how to handle closed doors and opportunities from God; how to apply physical, mental, and emotional habits; why we should forgive others; how I dealt with trauma; and how I came to recognize God's calling over my life. This will be a helpful book for your faith as a believer.

PART I

What Is
Prayer?

ONE

My Journey into Consistent Prayer

Holiday seasons have always been difficult for me. My mother experienced seasonal depression, so she always struggled during this time of year. Living in the Northwest, winters are dark, gloomy, and rainy. It's almost as if you can see the depression roll in with the dark clouds. Some of the most traumatic events I've experienced have occurred between Thanksgiving and the new year. Going into adulthood, I carried that baggage with me. As the winter holidays approached, feelings of anxiousness, sadness, and fear would emerge. To cope and feel a sense of comfort, I would isolate.

One year, a few days after Christmas, I experienced a particular mental episode that changed the trajectory of my life. I dropped my three sons off after my allotted parenting time, and I went back home feeling alone. My thoughts were too much to handle, so I retreated to self-medication in an attempt to escape from my invasive thoughts. What started as an attempt to relax soon became an overwhelming psychological ride that I wanted to jump off.

My mind was spiraling out of control as I sat remembering my failures, mistakes, and past. This led to self-sabotaging thoughts about my future decisions and the direction my life was heading. I was suffering through a drug-fueled anxiety attack as I was navigating the ups and downs of some extreme life changes. My breathing increased, and it felt as though my lungs were collapsing.

Leading up to this moment, I had experienced a divorce, had been recently released from prison, had been in and out of a couple short-term relationships, and was struggling with finding the purpose of my existence. While I had been incarcerated, I lost my business, which left me with little income. After I was released from prison, my only friend at the time moved in with me. The extra financial support was needed.

God knew what He was doing having my friend move in with me. He was a follower of Jesus, but he was never overbearing regarding his faith, and he never forced religion on me. He was always there when I needed to talk or had questions. I had given my life to Christ when I was seventeen, but I had spent over a decade running from a ministry calling and a prophetic word that had been spoken over my life. Although I knew who Jesus was, I hadn't talked to Him in a while, and I didn't know how to fully reconnect with Him.

In the middle of this paranoid panic attack, I remember running up the stairs and pounding on his door. It was the middle of the night, so he frantically opened the door thinking something was on fire or someone had been in an accident. When he opened the door, he stared at me with wide-open eyes. I was crying and trying to explain to him that I couldn't breathe. I was lost and needed answers, and my mind was swirling with crazy thoughts, irrational fears, and too many outcomes I couldn't wrap my head around. It was a mental breakdown the likes of which I had not experienced before, so I was pretty shaken up by it.

Hoping to calm me down, he asked if he could pray for me. I agreed. I was willing to try anything. He prayed with me right there on the spot, and I immediately felt the peace and comfort of God rush over me. My breath was restored, my mind stopped racing, and an indescribable peace came over me. I sat down at the top of the stairs, and I was able to gather myself and share with him my concerns, overpowering fears, and all the things that had me extremely anxious. He gently answered all my questions, helped deescalate my invasive thoughts, helped me gather myself, and sent me back to my room to get some rest. There was one burning question that I had to ask before going to bed.

"What should I do if this happens again?" I asked him.

His simple but powerful response was, "Pray to God. Communicate with Him and spend more time reading His Word." I went back to my bedroom with the answer I had been looking for. I needed God.

Immediately an overwhelming number of questions spread like wildfire through my mind. *Who really is God? Does He want to hear from me? Is He mad at me? Does He want to help me even though I'm not living a life that glorifies Him? Does He still love me?* Even amid these questions, I felt the gentle Holy Spirit reassure me that I could come as I was, and that God desired a relationship with me.

I lay down that night and knew what choices had to be made. For me, this mental breakdown was like hitting rock bottom. I was ready for a fresh start and ready to refocus all my attention onto Him and no longer on me. This was the last straw of doing things my way. My way had always failed me, my way had always left me feeling empty, and my way had always left me lost and confused.

Now that I had encountered the Holy Spirit, I knew trying to solve all my issues and troubles on my own was no longer the answer. From that day forward (although I have been far from perfect), I committed to be in constant communication with God through prayer, to be devoted to Scripture, and to truly surrender my life to Christ.

Right Result, Wrong Motive

When I first got saved, at the age of seventeen, I did it for all the wrong reasons. There was a girl I wanted to pursue, but her older brother said that I had to be a "Christian" in order to date her. Hoping he could reach me with the Gospel, he asked me to join him on a car ride. In the car, he boldly presented the Gospel of Jesus Christ to me for the very first time.

He explained what sin was and what the consequences of it were; about the separation between me and God; about the death, burial, and resurrection of Jesus Christ; and how to receive the free gift of salvation. In that moment, it made sense. I was a lost soul, and I needed a Savior. I was living in a pit of despair but celebrating a life filled with sin. Before this moment, I had lived with no awareness of sin, the consequences of sin, or even the consciousness of offending

God with how I lived. So, I accepted Jesus Christ as my Lord and Savior. That day marked the beginning of the end. The end of a life being lived blindly in opposition of a Holy and Perfect God. I repented from the life of debauchery, received the Holy Spirit, and accepted the free gift of salvation by putting my faith in Jesus.

After accepting Jesus into my life, sin never felt the same. It failed to satisfy, and I could see it for what it truly was—a counterfeit. I wish I could say that I experienced smooth sailing from that day forward and that I surrendered my life to Jesus all the rest of my days, but that's not how the story ends. In fact, that was just the beginning. The years after accepting Jesus into my heart brought many lessons that were defined by hurt, pain, hard revelations, and tribulations straight from the school of hard knocks. I had sincerely accepted Jesus, but I had done it with a wrong motive.

I moved forward in life not attending church, not being discipled, and not having Christian friends or mentors to provide guidance or to showcase how to live fully surrendered to God. I struggled to figure out what it was to be a Christian. My environment was the same. It was still filled with drugs, alcohol, violence, abuse, and immorality. I wasn't able to establish good practices or truly understand what it was to have a relationship with Jesus and follow Him. There wasn't anyone in my life to give me godly counsel and wisdom, and reading the Bible only confused me further. Although I had been set free, I didn't know where to start. I didn't know what being set free even meant. I had so many questions, and I was extremely lost.

I think a lot of people who didn't grow up in the church also find themselves in these moments of wondering what comes next. I said the prayer, I believe what I said, but how does this whole salvation thing work? Is life supposed to get easier? Do I get three wishes now? Am I still going to have hard times and troubles? When is this Jesus guy coming back anyway? It seemed as though accepting Christ was an urgent decision, and I thought my life afterward was going to be characterized by mountain-moving miracles. To my surprise, I went back home, and things were relatively the same.

Between the ages of seventeen and nineteen, my life was rough. It was filled with mistakes, failures, and visits to jail. Although I made my way to church at times, I never felt at home. I didn't fit in. At that time, the Christian culture and community seemed cliquey and seemed to emphasize living a perfect life free from sin. I never really found people who understood me. There wasn't much transparency of troubles and real-life issues displayed, and there wasn't openness or honesty. Since struggles weren't shared, it made it hard for me to relate to the Christian community. It seemed as if a bunch of hurt people were gathering together pretending that everything was good and putting on this great, elaborate show of a perfect life walking with Jesus. I couldn't relate.

I knew in my heart that I needed to be there because I was lost, broken, and in search of answers. This was a period in my life when I really understood what Paul was feeling when he wrote, "I do not understand the things I do. I do not do what I want to do, and I do the things I hate" (Romans 7:15 NCV). I was pulled between cultural norms and being Kingdom minded. I was being influenced by entertainment, music, my peers, and the world. As a young adult, it was very difficult to try to navigate the tightrope of what it meant to fit in and be successful and yet die to myself, pick up my cross, and follow Jesus.

The fact of the matter is that I had spent more time in the world than I had in the Word. I didn't know how to be a Christian, have a relationship with Jesus, pray, or understand the Bible. Many of my stances, opinions, and beliefs were grounded and rooted in worldly wisdom that included my past trauma and personal experiences. The world kept calling me and making me feel accepted, but the Holy Spirit kept trying to direct me away from the world. There was this constant battle between good and evil, the world and the Holy Spirit, and living for myself versus living for Jesus. The truth is that during this season of my life, my flesh won.

From Crisis Prayer to Consistent Prayer

When I was nineteen, I was sent to county jail. I started attending some of the church services they held every week. They called them "cookie church services" because the pastor showed up with a box of cookies for those who attended. It worked because I was drawn in. At first, I went just for the treats; however, the Word of God does not return void. I found myself looking forward to church, no longer for the cookies, but for the camaraderie, the brotherhood, and the peace that came with worshiping freely even while being locked inside of a cage. I started building the courage to communicate with God again. My communication with the Lord, however, was more of "If You do this, then I'll do that"–type prayers. Those prayers still reside in my memory.

"God, if You get me out of here, I promise I'll be good."

"God, if You cut my sentence short, I'll never come back to this place."

"God, if You let me out this week, I'll find a church and I'll serve You the rest of my life."

This is what I like to call crisis prayer. Crisis prayer is praying only to get something that I want, not what I need. It was only in the middle of a crisis that I communicated with God. I found myself bargaining with Him, trying to strong-arm Him, and trying to convince Him that if He let me out of jail, I would follow Him for the rest of my life. Even though my intentions weren't pure, God was still able to pull me out of my wishful thinking of getting out sooner and allowed me to feel His love and presence while in jail.

I started developing spiritual habits such as consistently praying, reading my Bible, attending church, and hanging out with the other inmates who did the same thing. I found myself less likely to get involved in all the negativity that comes with being incarcerated. I started analyzing what I was watching and consuming, and I began a journey of being more consistent and disciplined in my devotions. My foundation of consistency and discipline was built in jail. Eventually, I was released from county jail, and I carried on with my old ways and habits.

Years later, at the age of 25, I began attending church again. Although I'd love to say attending this church fully transformed me, I can't. When one of my prayers was answered, I left the church. Yes, my prayer was answered, so I left! I'd been praying for direction. I was asking God to answer me, to lead me, and to reveal to me why He had created me. One evening, an evangelist from this church pulled me out of the crowd and asked me to come up onstage. He had received a prophetic word from God about my calling. This was the answer I'd been praying for. I thought, *He's going to reveal to me why God created me and what the direction for my life is.*

The evangelist looked me in my eyes and said, "Andrew, you have been called to ministry. You have words of gold, and you're going to speak to millions of people about Jesus."

My ear-to-ear smile dropped. This was the worst news I had ever received. My heart's desire was to be delivered from the dead-end jobs I was working, to receive a promotion, to get a better high-paying job, to step into my million-dollar career, anything that would have an impact on my financial burden. I viewed ministry as a death sentence. The pastor of this church was a father of ten children, and he worked a full-time job in addition to his role in pastoral care. It sounded outrageous that I would live a lifestyle of telling people about Jesus and still be weighed down by life's problems. Although he was an amazing man, that was not the life I wanted. He was the only example I'd seen of what ministry looked like.

Although I received an answer to my long-awaited prayer, it left me disappointed, discouraged, and defeated. I left before I even gave it a chance. I ran for my life as far as my feet would take me—in the opposite direction of church. I left the church for years pursuing my own dreams, visions, and goals. I tried building my own kingdom.

One thing I did take away from attending this church, however, was valuable biblical context. They were very militant in their discipleship process. While being discipled and spending so much time studying the Word of God, I became familiar with Scripture, fasting, praying, and seeking His face. This is when I realized what building and having a relationship with God meant—the relationship between the Father and His child, me. I saw the results of consistently praying, and my desire for communication with Him grew stronger. Through prayer, I felt His loving presence. As a result of my prayer life, I watched God's hand move in situations and witnessed miracles take place.

As I made an effort to draw closer to God, He drew closer to me. As I started praying to Him every day, my prayers turned toward seeking His guidance, provision, and direction for my life. I took all my decisions, questions, and choices before His throne. I learned the true meaning of fellowship with the Creator of the universe. Coming to this realization was a beautiful time in my life that was characterized by a deeper and stronger understanding of who God is and who He says I am.

It was during this time that I learned that prayer is not an obligation. It is an absolute privilege to be able to speak to the One who created me. As God's children, we can have ongoing, open, honest, and transparent communication with the Creator of all things. We must stay in constant communication with Him so that He can continue to keep us in alignment with His plan and purpose for our lives. God answers our prayers, even if it's a *yes*, *no*, or *not right now*. We must accept His response to our prayers, because we know that He will never lead us astray and that He always has our best interests at heart.

This is part of my journey to a consistent prayer life. The more consistent you are with prayer, the more you're going to hear from Him. As you communicate with God and share your intimate thoughts and feelings with Him, your heart becomes more willing to listen and obey His directions. Prayer is the greatest communion form that we have with God, and it conforms our thoughts to His. Consistent prayer helps us to remain in unity with God. Pray for consistency and discipline in your walk with Christ.

PRAYER FOR CONSISTENCY

Heavenly Father, help me to be more consistent. I know that You are more concerned with my availability than my ability. Help me to set aside excuses, distractions, and anything that leads me to compromise. Give me the power to be moved by faith and not by my feelings. Help me to show up regardless of my circumstances, environment, and emotions. Renew the power of the Holy Spirit in me, and give me the strength to overcome any obstacles that are designed to pull my attention away from You. In Jesus' name, Amen.

APPLICATION

1. What are some ways you can be more consistent in your walk with Christ?
2. In what crisis in your life have you run to God?
3. What was the outcome?
4. What are some ways that being consistent will improve your relationship with God and with other people?
5. What value do you see in being consistent?

TWO

Prayer Basics

We've all heard the saying, "communication is key." I've always been told that communication is the foundation of any healthy relationship. With this imprinted as our cultural norm, we're aware that there are protocols and procedures to follow when communicating in a group setting. First impressions are extremely important. We understand the protocol for going to a job interview is not to high-five our interviewer and yell, "Let's go, let's get this job!" Instead, we enter the room, shake our interviewer's hand, and respectfully introduce ourselves. "Hello. I'm Andrew. Nice to meet you." There are formalities to which we adhere.

Similarly, building a friendship or a casual acquaintance requires clear and consistent communication. These communication skills ultimately lead to a successful, long-term relationship with a spouse, a friend, or family members.

When we enter into a relationship with God, the idea of prayer often becomes complicated. We know that communication is very important, but we often begin by following our cultural norms and protocols when we speak to God. That doesn't sound like an intimate relationship to me. In order to have an intimate relationship with God, we need to throw everything society has taught us about communication out the window. We need to get to a place where we feel completely free, comfortable, and vulnerable when we speak to Him.

When I'm talking to my wife, there aren't a lot of guidelines, boundaries, or rules. I speak to her openly, honestly, and with full transparency. I try to be vulnerable and speak straight from my feelings. I've found that the more open I am in my lines of communication, the deeper our bond becomes and the more confident I am in our relationship. I feel safe to share everything with her.

I believe God desires this kind of communication from us. He wants a relationship with us that is without boundaries or borders, one that is raw and real, one that is moved by passion and love, and one that never ends. Scripture tells us to "Pray without ceasing" (1 Thessalonians 5:17 NASB). This is one of the key elements of our prayer life. Conversations with God do not have a period; they have a comma. God wants us to have ongoing, intimate, and vulnerable conversations with Him daily.

Back to Basics

Let's get back to the basics of a prayer life. It's not complicated! After I first open my eyes in the morning, I immediately close them to connect with my heavenly Father. I thank Him for allowing me to experience another day, I thank Him for breathing breath into my lungs, and I praise

Him for His sovereignty, His love, His grace, and His mercy. Praying before going to bed at night is just as easy. My prayer before bed is thanking Him for another day. That rolls right into the very next morning, when I thank Him for a new day. It's literally a conversation that never ends and has no periods.

It's a privilege to communicate with the One who created you, so you have to remember to keep Him at the forefront of your heart when you wake up, as you journey throughout your day, and before you go to sleep. Thanking Him for waking you up and blessing you with another day is a simple way to show your gratitude. You can incorporate anything into your prayer that's on your heart.

One of my favorite ways to pray is getting down on my knees, folding my hands, and bowing my head. In fact, I make a practice of doing so at least twice a day throughout the day. We all pray in different ways and in different locations, whether that's in bed, on the floor, in the shower, in a prayer closet, in a vehicle, at the office, or at a store. Regardless of where you pray, if you're praying without ceasing, then there is not a right or wrong place to pray. Anywhere works! I'll pray while I'm getting ready, while I'm driving, or while I'm working out at the gym. I've prayed for people in the supermarket, on the streets, and over the phone. Praying without ceasing means anytime, anywhere, and in any way.

Even though we can pray at any moment, I still recommend having a designated place you can go to spend alone time with God. It is helpful to have a place where you can escape the noise of your environment and any distractions to enter into prayer. This will help strengthen your relationship so that you can feel His presence intimately.

My sanctuary happens to be my Jeep. I call it my spiritual tank. In my war room on wheels, I've held Bible studies, invited hundreds of people to follow Jesus, and created thousands of prayer videos for those who are embarking on their social media scroll journey. God put it on my heart to help bring people's attention back to Him, to get ahold of their focus, and to remind them that the Creator of the universe desires a relationship with them. My sanctuary allows me to get alone with God and feel His presence, which then allows the Holy Spirit to lead me in my line of ministry work.

Digital Missionary

My mission and passion will always be to bring people back to a place of connection with God. Social media is a great place to do that; however, I've experienced some controversy when it comes to my public prayer videos. The criticism typically comes from well-meaning Christians who highlight the Scripture verse that says, "But when you pray, go into your room and shut the door and pray to your Father who is in secret. And your Father who sees in secret will reward you" (Matthew 6:6 ESV). What many believe is that praying on social media, praying in public, or praying anywhere that's not behind a closed door is self-seeking, self-glorifying, and against the Word of God.

Jesus Himself had a very intentional public ministry. He prayed for people while He was in the public eye. He spoke parables to large gatherings, and He performed miracles and healed the sick in front of people. When we read Matthew 6:6, we have to understand the context. Jesus was talking

32

about the Pharisees who enjoyed putting on a public display of their faith for self-seeking reasons. They would put themselves on a pedestal and put together elaborate and lengthy prayers that were only for show (see Matthew 6:5). These religious leaders were more concerned with the outer appearance and what people thought of them than they were with the salvation of mankind. Jesus could see right through their schemes, and He knew their true heart posture. Jesus called them hypocrites for doing this.

Early in my digital missionary work, I allowed critical comments to get to me. But as I grounded myself in deep prayer with the Lord, He reminded me that He is able to use these prayers to redirect people's attention back to Him through social media platforms. The very place that is telling us to follow the things of this world, our Creator is using for His Kingdom. God wants to meet people right where they're at. He's able to reach people all around the world through Christian content creators like myself who are bold enough to put themselves out there, who are not afraid of criticism, and who love God's people enough to be the front-runners to help save souls.

Sharing vulnerable and meaningful prayers with people can help them navigate their prayer lives with God. What makes for a meaningful prayer is the posture of the heart. Are you saying the prayer out of obligation, or are you saying the prayer understanding that it is a privilege to talk with God? Sometimes we can think of prayer as a burden or an inconvenience in our schedule. Sometimes we think it isn't effective because of the lack of tangible results.

If you're feeling this way, I would recommend the following practice when praying. Position yourself in a posture of worship by kneeling with your head down and humbling yourself before the King. When I implemented this into my prayer life, it made the largest impact. As it says in the book of James, "God is against the proud, but he gives grace to the humble" (James 4:6 NCV).

While you can pray anywhere, anytime, in any manner, some prayers require a deeper level of intimacy. Sometimes prayers need extra communication time, a quiet environment, a different mindset, and an intentional position of praise. We must remind ourselves that there is no prayer too small or too big for God. He desires intimacy with us that's so deep that we bring Him into every aspect of our lives knowing we can't do life without Him. Getting to this place in your relationship with Him requires humility and an understanding that's larger than life. God cares about the smallest and finest details of your life.

Getting Consistent

Consistency has shaped my life, not just in prayer and communication with God but in every aspect such as physical, emotional, and even financial health. The bridge between where you're at today and where you want to be is consistency. There's power in consistently choosing to be disciplined, even in small ways.

One aspect of a healthy relationship is trust. Trust is built from experience, which means being reliable and showing up. When we consistently show up in prayer day in and day out, we start learning how to trust God. We can rely on Him to meet us wherever we are and whenever we call on Him. In other words, the more we talk to God, the more we hear from Him. The more we hear from Him, the more we trust Him, and the healthier our relationship with Him becomes.

Being consistent can be challenging because we live in a results-driven world. We live in a microwave generation. People want what they want, and they want it immediately. They want the seven-hour, warm, savory, home-cooked meal but in thirty seconds. Many times, Christians mistake their relationship with God with having a personal genie. If they rub the magic lamp, God will snap His fingers and deliver their wish to them on a golden platter. When what they pray for doesn't come to pass, they feel God doesn't love them or He's not listening to them. God is a God of provision. As it says in the Bible, "My God will meet all your needs according to the riches of his glory in Christ Jesus" (Philippians 4:19). He will provide what you need, not always what you want.

God is the Creator of the universe and knows what's best for you. Many people find it hard to consistently show up in prayer because after praying for something a few times, God answers them with a *no* or *not right now*, and they give up. Many people will say, "Jesus, take the wheel," but when He's not steering them in the direction they want to go, they snatch the wheel right back and start steering themselves. Taking control!

When you understand that prayer doesn't always result in what you want but that God will provide what you need, you show up consistently regardless of whether or not the results met your expectations. I consistently show up in prayer because I want to check in with the Author of my soul, I want to hear from the One who goes before me, and I want to spend time with the One who knows the number of hairs on my head. When you consistently show up in prayer regardless of the results, you start to get to know His voice, how He operates, and how He answers your prayers in love. You have established a trusting relationship because you know you can trust His guidance.

Feel the Flow

In eighth grade, I fell in love with the game of basketball. Michael Jordan was at the height of his career, and it was his final year of his last championship run with the Chicago Bulls. I was immersed in basketball culture, from Kobe Bryant to Allen Iverson and Kevin Garnett. I was in love. The problem was, I wasn't that good at it. There were physical setbacks I had to fix in order to for me to be able to play basketball, and I was determined to repair my health.

Previously the heaviest kid in class, I lost weight to pass conditioning. I still dealt with residual effects of having underdeveloped lungs as a child, so I strengthened my lungs by practicing breathing techniques and exercising. I spent all of my waking hours on the court playing basketball or at home watching basketball on television. As my love for the game grew, I got more competent at it and started to realize I would never be a great one-on-one player.

I was built to be a team player. I was a valuable asset because I was reliable, I ran the plays, I played great team ball, and I excelled at communicating. Great basketball teams excel in communication both verbally and nonverbally. There's an intricate flow to the game when five players are on the court at one time. They understand how each other operates, they

36

know what the other one is thinking, and they know what the next move is that they're going to make without having to say a word. How is this possible? The answer is that they spend a lot of time together. The order of operation is a beautiful thing to watch. It's like poetry in motion in which everybody is in alignment with one another.

Having a constant flow of communication with God is similar. The more time you spend in His presence, in His Word, and with His people, the more familiar you become with the Holy Spirit and how He operates within you. You sense His nudges and urges, and you can see the direction He's leading you. You have a better understanding of how He operates and how He orchestrates situations in your life. There's a flow. It's almost like a dance between you and your Creator. Establishing this personal and unique flow between you and God may be hard, but the more time you spend and connect with Him, the easier it becomes to feel the flow.

Here's a prayer tip. If you want to get to a place where you're comfortable praying, you should watch other mighty, God-fearing men and women who pray boldly. Listen to how they pray and the things they pray about. Use their prayers as an outline or guide for your prayers. I became a better basketball player by watching how my favorite professional athletes played. I found myself using their plays but with my own moves.

It's the same with prayer. Spend time with other Spirit-filled believers and listen to the way they pray and interact with God. Pay attention to how they act, how they dance with God, and how they communicate with Him. Take notes and adopt some of their practices. Over time you will develop your own relationship that flows beautifully and that will eventually inspire others to dance with God.

The Bible is a beautiful picture painted by the Creator of the universe. It's a love letter personally written for us that details how to reestablish a connection with the One we were separated from because of our sin. "All Scripture is breathed out by God and profitable for teaching, for reproof, for correction, and for training in righteousness, that the man of God may be complete, equipped for every good work" (2 Timothy 3:16–17 ESV). The Bible teaches us how to talk with God. It has the ability to correct us, to train us, and to equip us so that we're complete and lack nothing.

The Bible is the greatest influence in my life and has had the most impact on my prayer life and relationship with God. It's filled with wisdom, powerful prayers, and stories of those who have gone before us, both men and women, who developed intimate relationships with God. I reflect on the book of Psalms, where David, a man after God's own heart, goes on emotional rants filled with highs and lows. But he always put his confidence in God.

While most of his stories start from a place of despair, hurt, betrayal, pain, and being overwhelmed, he closes many of his passages by saying he will not be shaken, that his faith is intact, and his trust is in the Lord. He knew that if God had done it once before, He certainly will do it again. If you struggle with redirecting your focus back onto God when you're facing difficulties, it's time to reevaluate your current habits, prune and audit some things in your life that are pulling at your attention, and start forming a consistent prayer life. Prayer is your line of defense against attacks.

PRAYER FOR REFINEMENT

Father God, reveal to me the areas in my life that require a change. Break any habits that I have outgrown, and shake me free from any ruts I've gotten myself stuck in. Search my heart with Your holy light and bring them to the surface. Show me all the things that need to be pruned, cut, or audited. Refine me and use Your Holy Scripture to whittle away the rough edges of my character. Help me to stay focused, consistent and disciplined. In Jesus' name, Amen.

APPLICATION

1. What does your current prayer life look like?
2. How would others describe your style of communication? How does that differ from your approach to communication with God? To what degree is it effective, and what needs to change?
3. What are some things you can prune and audit in your life that are distracting you from connecting with God?
4. What does a healthy prayer life look like to you? What small changes can you make today to create a healthier prayer life?

THREE

A Biblical Template for Prayer

Some of my early discipleship training came from well-meaning brothers in Christ who I met in jail when I was eighteen. Their love, passion, and knowledge stuck with me. Many of them had been in and out of jail and yet had held on to their faith.

One biblical devotion I took with me when I left jail was a daily proverb study guide. The book of Proverbs has thirty-one chapters. A long month in the year also has thirty-one days. The core men who participated in this curriculum would gather each evening in one of our cells and read the corresponding chapter number from the book of Proverbs. If it was May 19th, we would read the nineteenth chapter of Proverbs.

It was also brought to my attention that there are one hundred and fifty Psalms in the Bible. When divided by the average days in a month, that equals reading five chapters in the book of Psalms a day. Being incarcerated, we had extra time on our hands. Those who wanted to strengthen their faith would come join us to read a chapter of Proverbs and five chapters of Psalms. In closing, we would recite the Lord's Prayer found in Matthew 6.

As a young man who had recently accepted Jesus, I hadn't received any formal discipleship, had zero leadership from youth camps or Sunday school, and had no connections with Christian organizations. Yet, the criminals who were in and out of jail were the first followers of Christ to teach me how to read my Bible. The seeds they planted helped me to better understand how to break down and absorb context from the Bible. I also understood quickly that the Lord's Prayer isn't something we just recite. It's a template that Jesus gave us for communicating with God.

> "And when you pray, do not heap up empty phrases as the Gentiles do, for they think that they will be heard for their many words. Do not be like them, for your Father knows what you need before you ask him. Pray then like this."
>
> Matthew 6:7–9 ESV

It doesn't say to pray these words exactly or to repeat His prayer, but rather to pray *like* this. We are to take Jesus' words, use them as a template, and have a conversation with God in our own unique way. Rather than recite the same thing over and over, we are to understand what it is that Jesus is saying and then speak to God from our heart.

Here's an example of how I see it. Imagine if I expressed the way I love my wife by reading her a Hallmark card.

Then I continued reading that same card to her every day. Not only would she know I'm not putting any thought, energy, and effort behind these words, but she wouldn't truly know the deep appreciation, love, and passion I have for her. Going through motions like this is not genuine, and it lacks intimacy. It wouldn't be personal or heartfelt. It's easy to memorize or repeat something that somebody else has already written, but if our words are going to be authentic, they must come from us and not a recited message. God wants us to communicate with Him authentically and from a genuine heart. He's not impressed by our ability to recite a Scripture verse or prayer that was written. Even though these practices may have their place, a real relationship must go deeper than that.

The Lord's Prayer that Jesus taught reads:

> "Our Father in heaven,
> hallowed be your name,
> your kingdom come,
> your will be done,
> on earth as it is in heaven.
> Give us today our daily bread.
> And forgive us our debts,
> as we also have forgiven our debtors.
> And lead us not into temptation,
> but deliver us from the evil one."
>
> Matthew 6:9–13

When we break down the elements of this prayer, we gain clarity about what an effective prayer is and how to communicate with God. In this passage, we learn the six key elements of effective prayer: honor, submission, provision, repentance, guidance, and protection. As you follow this template consistently, you will discover greater effectiveness in your spiritual life and deeper intimacy with God.

Honor the Lord

When Jesus enters into communication with God, He starts with, "Our Father in heaven, hallowed be your name." He is showing us that we need to enter prayer with honor, reverence, and respect for the holiness of God, understanding that He is our Father. It is a privilege to speak with the One who created us. He is a very good and just God who deserves glory, honor, and praise. If Jesus, who is God in the flesh, reveres and honors His name to initiate communication, then we should, too.

When we honor God, we're not only praising Him for His goodness, love, mercy, and grace, but we're also presenting humbly that we cannot live without Him. He is the Highest Authority in Heaven and on earth. The power of His name can heal us, save us, and protect us. When we approach God with the honor He deserves, our prayers start to sound different. Remind yourself that it's a privilege to be in communion with God. You're standing on holy ground. Honor the space and treat Him with respect.

Submission to God's Will

"Your kingdom come, your will be done" is telling us to be expectant of God's Kingdom and to submit to His will. When we come to an understanding that God's will is greater than our own, we're able to discern that what we want and

44

what we need are two different things. When we lay down our selfish desires and requests at the foot of His throne, we're actively submitting to His sovereign will. We are letting Him know we trust Him and want to follow His will, not our own. If things aren't going our way, they're going God's way, and that's the way things should go.

When we can identify who we are in Christ, who God is, and what the role is that we play in the larger scope of things, we start to desire God's will over everything. When it comes to health, finances, relationships, healing, miracles, or any aspect of my life, if it's not God's will, I don't want it. Sometimes that comes with grief, pain, suffering, and hurt, but I understand that it's better to go down the path He's laid out before me than to travel on my own path without the provision, protection, and direction He provides. Not submitting to God's will has only led me to destruction, damage, and a lack of purpose.

The Provision of God

"Give us today our daily bread" indicates that we should not have a preoccupation with tomorrow. We understand that yesterday has come and gone, and there's nothing we can do to change what has happened. Tomorrow has its own set of issues, worries, and obstacles. We know, however, that Jesus is already there making a way for us. We're called to focus on today while knowing that tomorrow isn't promised. With the twenty-four hours we're blessed with each day, we often spend those hours worrying, stressing, and focusing on things that haven't even happened yet. Many times, we're so preoccupied with tomorrow that we miss out on what

God is trying to do in our lives today. We get caught up in irrational fears, and we don't understand that our situation might not be as bad as we think.

This reminds me of the Israelites when they were freed from captivity of the Egyptians (see Exodus 13:17–14:31). God led them through the wilderness and provided for them daily by giving them bread from Heaven, quail meat, and water (see Exodus 16:11–12). Anything they stored up and tried to save for the next day began to rot and create an odor (see Exodus 16:19–20). But every day, God would supply a new batch of food that was exactly what they needed.

This story is a perfect reminder that you're not promised tomorrow, so don't spend today stressing over things that are out of your control. When you're praying, God already knows what you need, and He's going to make sure that you have it. If you don't have something, you don't need it to complete whatever His plan, purpose, and will is for that day.

True Repentance

The next verse speaks of repentance, which involves recalling any areas in which we have failed, missed the mark, or messed up. It says, "And forgive us our debts, as we also have forgiven our debtors." Keeping a log of all the ways we've sinned isn't necessary for salvation, but it helps us keep a clean conscience and clean heart so that we can let things go and move forward.

Practicing repentance daily is important. We can apply this when we're praying by reflecting on any area where we might have stepped out of alignment with God or overlooked a situation. When we realize our error, we ask for forgiveness.

To add to this, we lift up in prayer those who have hurt us, betrayed us, turned their back on us, or sinned against us. We should be praying for our brothers and sisters and anyone who has wronged us. It shows our level of maturity, and it shows that we are focused on the task at hand instead of being preoccupied with holding on to things and seeking revenge. We don't want to carry around baggage from failed situations; instead, we want to focus on creating and cultivating a relationship with God and fulfilling the purpose and plan for which God created us.

Daily Guidance

Jesus shows us that praying for divine guidance and direction from the Holy Spirit is an essential part of our walk with God. He says, "And lead us not into temptation." It's important that we ask God to help us navigate through what this world throws at us. We need our Heavenly Tour Guide so that we don't wander off. I often ask God to illuminate the path that He would have me go down. He will put us in the places He desires and in the places that align with His plan. I don't want to go where God hasn't called me to go.

For others, that's not always the case. Sometimes it's hard for people to stay on track. They follow their feelings and emotions that lead them on their own trail, and they work for results that satisfy. They lack patience. They want to be successful *now*. They want a family *now*. They want their business to grow *now*. They want their spouse *now*. They want to have a legacy *now*.

What I've found is that many times where the Spirit leads us isn't the path or direction we anticipated. Many times, it's either new territory to cross or it's a path less traveled with obstacles and challenges. This is why we must pray for guidance and direction daily. There will be traps and distractions disguised as opportunities that are meant to lead you off the path that God has laid out in front of you. The enemy wants nothing more than for you to get side-tracked, distracted, or comfortable on a path that looks appealing but leads you nowhere. When you ask God for guidance, you will receive actual guidance. If you're paying attention to the signs, He opens and closes doors right before your eyes.

God's Protection

Jesus prayed, "Deliver us from the evil one." Praying to be delivered from evil is not only praying for protection from evil but reminding ourselves of the finished work Jesus did on the cross that delivered us from our sins. We have a strong Deliverer who has already won the battle. The Bible says, "No weapon formed against you shall prosper" (Isaiah 54:17 NKJV). We can feel peace and comfort knowing that the enemy cannot touch us. We have been delivered from evil because of what Jesus did for us.

Asking God to protect you doesn't mean you won't experience obstacles, trials, tragedy, or bad news. The truth is that you will still experience pain, hurt, grief, loss, disappointment, and sadness. As life carries on, so will life's events. Asking God for protection means holding on to the fact that the things the enemy uses to try to destroy you will not last. His weapons can disrupt your plans, visions, dreams, and goals, but they can't stop what God has planned for you.

Weapons will form, but they won't prosper in the Spirit and within the scope of eternity. They will fail.

We pray for protection as a reminder that regardless of what we experience, God can use it for His good and His glory. We embrace struggle and hold on to the truth that all the evil formed can't change or shake what Jesus already did. We're secure in our salvation. This is a truth that should encourage us and bring us joy that the world doesn't have. As we stand firm in our foundation in Christ, evil can't rattle us.

PRAYER USING THE LORD'S PRAYER

God in Heaven, You are holy. I lay down all my dreams, visions, and goals at the foot of Your throne. I am thankful that Your plan, purpose, and will for my life will come to pass and always exceed my expectations. Lord, You know my need. I ask that You continue to sustain me and that my heart would remain grateful for all the things that You provide. I ask that You forgive me for all my mistakes, failures, and shortcomings. Help me to overlook the offenses of others that are done to me. I ask that You would close doors that are not from You and that You would lead me down the path You've laid out for me. I pray that You would protect me from the plots and schemes of the enemy that look to distract me and pull my attention and focus away from You. This life is not mine, as I'm just a vessel for Your works. Help me to use the breath that You breathe into my lungs to bring glory and honor to Your name. In Jesus' name, Amen.

APPLICATION

1. In which key areas of prayer can you make the most improvement? In which area of prayer do you spend the most time? Why?

2. Create your own prayer based on the key elements given to us by Jesus. Take some time to put it into your own words. What does a prayer that covers these areas look like for you?

PART II

What Hinders Your Prayer Life and How to Fix It

FOUR

Combating Feelings with Truth and Authenticity

Feelings are emotions and sensations that come from your perception of an experience. While they are valid, feelings are tied to our human nature. There have been many times I've allowed my feelings and emotions to get the best of me. This has happened to the point that those feelings blurred my understanding of who I was and to whom I belonged. I would make assumptions about situations based on my past experiences, traumas, doubts, and faults. Acting on my feelings and emotions was not Christlike. I didn't seek counsel from God before I reacted to things. I responded out of pain when I should have been responding out of love.

Growing up mixed-race in a non-diverse, predominantly white city, I was the only kid at my school who experienced racism, criticism, and gossip because of my skin color and hair texture. I stuck out like a sore thumb, and every day someone had something to say to me. From childhood to adulthood, not much changed except that I stuck out even more. I grew to six feet four, had a strong athletic build, had clean-cut curly hair, and got tattoos all over my body.

When I went out in public, people would either stare at me or whisper to each another as I walked past them. People assumed I was a professional athlete, a famous rapper, an actor, or gang affiliated. Even after I became a father of three and would go grocery shopping for dinner, I was still profiled based on my appearance. The idea of going out in public made me feel uncomfortable. Even though I never really knew what people were thinking, their staring felt like judgment. That judgment bred insecurity and intimidation.

There was one incident that forever changed my perspective of feeling judged by people. One day after leaving church, I went to Target to grab some snacks. I was wearing a shirt that read, "God is Dope." I was in my early thirties, had just started attending church again, and was working on my relationship with God. I wanted to wear a shirt that shared my faith. As usual, the stares, glares, and whispers began the moment I entered the store.

As I was walking around pushing my shopping cart, I noticed an older woman giving me a blank stare and showing no emotion. I felt uncomfortable, so I smiled at her and immediately looked away. She started pushing her shopping cart toward me, which made me feel nervous. I allowed my emotions to get the best of me. The fact that an older woman staring at me made me feel nervous and overwhelmed indicates I was projecting past traumas onto this situation.

The closer she got, the more I felt she was going to say something negative to me. As our carts neared one another and she was about to pass me, she looked up at me with a smile and said, "God is dope," and gave me a thumbs-up. The tension I felt released instantly, and I smiled back at her, feeling acceptance and love from a stranger in my town for the first time.

Prejudging this woman and fearing what might happen only caused me to feel anxiety, frustration, and discomfort. It was in this moment that I realized that I needed to learn how to take hold of my feelings and emotions and not allow them to dictate my actions, thoughts, or behaviors. While warranted, feelings are fleeting, and they don't always reflect reality. Feelings are interactive emotions we can't ignore because we express them every day; however, learning how to pause before we react is important. Don't allow your feelings to trap you into thinking your emotionally generated opinion is right. This is where faith and truth come in.

Truth over Feelings

Jesus laid out the blueprint for how we should handle our feelings. He experienced the full range of emotions including betrayal, humiliation, sadness, grief, and pain. He's the ultimate example of allowing Himself to feel but still making choices and decisions based on truth rather than emotion. The shortest verse in the Bible says, "Jesus wept" (John 11:35), and it describes Jesus' reaction when His friend Lazarus died. Even though He knew the truth of the miracle He was about to perform (bringing Lazarus back to life), He was overwhelmed with grief. In another example, Jesus experienced betrayal when Judas, one of His disciples, turned Jesus in to the Roman officials in exchange for some silver coins.

As Jesus prayed in the Garden of Gethsemane and prepared to carry the weight of the world's sins, Scripture tells us that He experienced deep sorrow (see Matthew 26:36–39). He even asked God to take the cup of suffering from Him. When Jesus was arrested in the Garden of Gethsemane, all His disciples fled—even though they had proclaimed they would die for Him and always be with Him. Jesus felt sorrow, disappointment, loneliness, betrayal, sadness, pain and many other emotions that we do.

By reading the Bible, we learn what Jesus went through and how He handled His emotions and feelings. The fact that God came to earth as flesh reassures us that He knows exactly how we feel when we go through difficult situations. He gave us His Son to look to as an example of how to handle things righteously. Jesus felt deep emotions but always came back to the truth, purpose, plan, and will of God. He embraced suffering with His eyes on eternity and focused on the greater outcome.

As you navigate through feelings, it is important you don't let them take your focus off God or lead you astray. Feelings can be very distracting. A verse I look to for confirmation, regardless of what I'm going through, is Romans 8:28: "And we know that for those who love God all things work together for good, for those who are called according to his purpose" (ESV). He orchestrates everything together for good, including hard times, closed doors, rejection, and events that activate our emotions.

As we face emotion-triggering events, we choose to *respond* or to *react*. A knee-jerk reaction is an automatic and predictable reaction that is often done without thinking. These types of reactions usually come from the flesh. It's the way that we react when we don't allow the Holy Spirit to breathe life into the situation. When we choose to respond instead of reacting, however, we allow extra time for us to be able to activate a God-filled response. This kind of response is well thought out and prayed over.

Let's see how this might play out in a situation you might face.

You're having a hectic morning and are running late for work. You get in your car and start driving faster than you normally would. As you try to get into the left lane to make a left turn, a driver cuts you off and veers into your lane without putting on his blinker. To avoid an accident, you're forced to go straight instead of making your left turn. Your heart is pounding, and in that moment, you have a choice to make. Do you react by laying on the horn? Do you yell out the window? Do you use special hand signals to express yourself? Or do you take a deep breath, focus on the road ahead of you, and continue to work safely?

I'd hazard a guess that the vast majority would have a knee-jerk reaction—we would at least honk our horn to vent our frustration. It is these smaller moments in our lives that we may not think are significant enough to change our character, but they do. It's the accumulation of these smaller, day-to-day situations in which we are not good representations of Jesus that can lead to further problems. If we let our flesh lead us, we will start letting our feelings and emotions lead our life. This approach will not produce fruit. In fact, it can dim our light and reduce our overall resolution and happiness.

Now let's examine the same scenario from the perspective of the driver who cut you off. He's a single father who doesn't know Jesus. He's a man hanging on to life by a thread. He makes a mistake by cutting you off because he's rushing to get his kids dropped off at school. You honk your horn and drive by him grumbling. He's disappointed in himself yet again. He's fed up. He's tired of making the same mistakes in his life. He goes home and decides to end his life.

While this may seem extreme, a single reaction from one person can alter the course of another person's life. It's so easy to allow our flesh to motivate us based on our feelings, environment, and circumstances that we become unaware and react to everything that happens to us. We're not allowing ourselves to have a God-filled response. In Scripture, we're instructed to be led by the Holy Spirit, who dwells in us knowing that in those moments we're having an impact in the Kingdom of Heaven.

> For those who live according to the flesh set their minds on the things of the flesh, but those who live according to the Spirit set their minds on the things of the Spirit. For to set the mind on the flesh is death, but to set the mind on the Spirit is life and peace. For the mind that is set on the flesh is hostile to God, for it does not submit to God's law; indeed, it cannot. Those who are in the flesh cannot please God.
>
> Romans 8:5–8 ESV

The Word of God is very clear that when we are led by our flesh and our minds are set on the things of this world, we are hostile to God. We cannot please God if we live a life led by reaction. We must not allow ourselves to be moved by every feeling, emotion, and change in our circumstances. When we are led by the Holy Spirit and allow ourselves to pause and pray before we respond, our lives are led to life and peace. We have to be diligent and careful about what we fill our minds with so that we can respond prayerfully and protect our peace.

Our feelings will mislead us every time. We are allowed to embrace our feelings as we encounter different trials, tribulations, obstacles, and storms; however, we must handle those feelings as Jesus would. He understood the cost of fulfilling His purpose and the cost that came with God's will being done—an element of suffering. But His faith wasn't dependent on earthly fame or worldly victory. His eyes were set on the eternal glory that would come from seeing His Father's plan all the way through. In the same way, we must separate ourselves from our suffering and remember that it's not about us.

The Word of God tells us to focus on heavenly things. Our faith is not of this world, and our hope is not in earthly success. We received the greatest gift when we put our faith in Jesus—the free gift of salvation. If that's the only gift God ever gives us, then He has given us everything we need to complete our journey on this earth (see 2 Peter 1:3). We have to start looking at life through the lens of the Lord and realize that life is not about us. The world tells us to follow our heart and do what makes us happy. The Word of God doesn't say that!

We are to follow God, not our heart. Our heart is deceitful and doesn't know what to do when we experience hurt and pain that evokes certain feelings. When we follow God, however, He will be with us through it all (see Deuteronomy 31:8). It should give us hope to know that Jesus experienced the full range of emotions and still accomplished God's will so that we could have access to God. That hope can get us through whatever this world throws at us. We have to put our faith over our feelings.

Don't Let the Enemy Win

The enemy is the father of lies, the accuser of the brethren, and the great deceiver. He will manipulate Scripture, lie, and create division to lead you astray. He uses your feelings and emotions to take your focus off Jesus. He's after your identity. He doesn't want you to know who you are and the power you have. The enemy comes to distract you, lie to you, use your feelings and emotions against you, derail you, and make you feel unworthy. When you're already relying on yourself instead of the Holy Spirit, the enemy doesn't have to work as hard to tear you down. When we start anchoring ourselves in the truth, the enemy has to work overtime.

In the book of Matthew, we read the story of Jesus inviting Peter to step out of the boat and walk to Him on the water. Jesus encouraged Peter to have faith and trust that He could do the impossible. "Then Peter got down out of the boat, walked on the water and came toward Jesus. But when he saw the wind, he was afraid and, beginning to sink, cried out, 'Lord, save me!'" (Matthew 14:29–30). For a moment, Peter had his eyes focused on Jesus. Because of that, he did what no man had ever done—he stepped out of the boat onto water. It wasn't until Peter took his focus off Jesus and started focusing on his environment that he began to sink. Peter allowed his feelings of inadequacy, fear, unbelief, and lack of authority to move him, causing him to be shakable and movable.

This is a monumental teaching for us. We start out with our eyes focused on Jesus, then the enemy starts using our environment, circumstances, and emotions against us to distract us. If we're not grounded and anchored in truth, we will easily be distracted. We will start to become overwhelmed and anxious. We will start to make assumptions and jump to conclusions without the proper foundation. We will get off track and find ourselves sinking from our own unbelief.

Conversely, when we stand on the truth of God's Word, we are immovable and have an unshakable and firm foundation on which to build our lives. We are no longer tossed around on the waves of the ocean. The enemy may be the father of lies, but the opposite of a lie is the truth, and the truth will set you free!

This is the truth:

- You are more than a conqueror (see Romans 8:37).
- The power in you is greater than the power in this world (see Luke 10:19).
- You have been chosen and set aside (see 1 Peter 2:9).
- God has a plan to prosper you (see Jeremiah 29:11).
- You are a friend of God (see John 15:15).
- God formed you in your mother's womb, and He knows the number of hairs on your head (see Psalm 139:13–16).
- God goes before you (see Isaiah 45:2).
- God prepares good works for you to complete (see Ephesians 2:10).

Because of the death, burial, and resurrection of Jesus Christ, you no longer have to allow your feelings, emotions, and flesh to lead you astray. You are no longer bound by these chains. Tell the enemy that he has no authority over you, your mind, your heart, your body, or your soul. Stand on the truth of your faith and allow God to lead you in the direction of His plan, purpose, and will for which He created you. God wants you to come as you are and experience the full freedom that comes with His free gift of salvation.

PRAYER FOR DISCERNING TRUTH

Father God, thank You for Your truth. Thank You for Your love, and thank You for defining who I am. Lord, today I choose to stand on my faith rather than on my feelings. Help me to be slow to speak and quick to listen. Help me to seek after understanding more than being understood. Help me to be led by the Spirit in all of my responses, and help me to use every interaction to bring glory to Your name. Help me to remember that I'm an ambassador for You, a light in this world, and a torchbearer for the truth. I am honored and privileged to share the Good News with those I encounter. Help me to do so today in truth and in love. In Jesus' mighty name, Amen.

APPLICATION

1. How have your feelings and emotions led you astray or misguided you in the past?
2. What are some practical ways you can exercise responding rather than reacting?

3. There's power in Scripture. This week, take time each day to write on a sticky note one verse that has a powerful truth about your identity in Christ or the true nature of God. Place the notes strategically in places you'll see as little reminders and recite them throughout the day. Each week, switch out your notes with new verses. This is a great way to stand on truth and write Scripture on your heart.

FIVE

Turning from Sin Toward Repentance and a Pure Heart

We are born into sin, and our sins separate us from God. Being born into sin makes it impossible for us to have a relationship with the Creator of the universe. "For all have sinned and fall short of the glory of God" (Romans 3:23). It's not a surprise to Him that we're imperfect. He knew we needed a Savior. A payment needed to be made for the penalty of our sins so that order would be restored and the gap between us and God would be closed. This was the sacrifice of God's Son who died on the cross for our sins. Because of what Jesus accomplished on the cross, the veil was torn, the sin that separated us from God was removed, and our relationship with God was restored.

This unimaginable sacrifice is why we put our faith in Jesus and accept Him as our Lord and Savior. Jesus said, "I am the way and the truth and the life. No one comes to the Father except through me" (John 14:6). This is the free gift of salvation, and it means that there is no amount of good works you can perform that will buy your way into Heaven. We are saved by grace, not by works (see Ephesians 2:8–9). Once you fully acknowledge who Jesus is and what He's done for you, you start turning from your old ways of sin and heading down a path that honors and glorifies Jesus.

Living a life that brings honor and glory to Him includes repenting from our sins. Jesus said, "I have not come to call the righteous, but sinners to repentance" (Luke 5:32). When we repent from our sins, we declare out of our mouths that we know we have sinned and truly ask God to forgive us. This allows God to restore and purify our hearts. When we repent from our sins, we're acknowledging that a change needs to be made in our mind and heart about something we know we've done that is not Christlike. Maybe it was how we reacted to something, what we said behind someone's back, what we did in private, what lies we told, or other actions that are not good representations of Jesus. It takes a sincere change of mind to repent and pursue righteousness again. You used to think one way, and now you think the exact opposite.

Repentance is a great illustration of what happens when you come to Jesus. Before you knew Him, you followed your own ways and your own thoughts. But once you had a divine revelation of who Jesus is, you turned and headed in the opposite direction of your ways. You started following Him and making better decisions. As you changed your mind and heart, your actions began to follow. You realized the way that you were living and the things you had been doing did not line up with God's plan. Your ideas, behaviors, beliefs, and opinions about things begin to change.

Repenting from your sins is a divine heart-posture checkup to remind yourself that you can always do better.

Transformation Takes Time

For many people, this isn't an overnight transformation. When I was seventeen, I accepted Jesus Christ as my Lord and Savior. At the time, I did repent of my sins; however, after accepting Him into my heart, my unhealthy environment didn't change. No one took me under his or her wing and taught me how to live a righteous life. I was young, and I continued down the path I was on before. I continued to follow the adults and peers in my life who thought toxic environments were normal. I kept doing drugs, drinking alcohol, and engaging in sexual activities.

The only thing that changed after I accepted Christ was that sinful behavior no longer satisfied. My conscience, prompted by the Holy Spirit, would warn me every time I did something inherently wrong by making me feel guilt or regret. This triggered heavy and overwhelming emotions. After I accepted Christ, I could no longer live a life that was full of sin without feeling severe conviction. For years, I was constantly burdened by my actions and behaviors.

It wasn't until over a decade later, after fully surrendering to the Lord and the truth of God's Word, that I saw Jesus' light shining on the dark areas of my life. I could've been healed years sooner if I hadn't been stubborn, if I had repented from my sins, and if I had taken the time to learn how to be obedient to convictions. If you delay repenting from your sins, your sin will get stronger and cause your heart to harden. "For all have sinned and fall short of the glory of God" (Romans 3:23). God wants to purify your heart and has promised you forgiveness.

Sanctification is the process of being made holy and set apart for special use. As believers, we go through three phases of sanctification. First, we are separated from the penalty of sin through justification. Second, we're separated from the power of sin through spiritual maturity. Third, we're separated from the presence of sin through glorification.

The moment you give your life to Christ and invite the Holy Spirit to dwell inside of you, you become a child of God and a follower of Jesus. From that day forward, the process of sanctification is moving you toward glorification, which is the permanent and ultimate holiness we will experience at the end of our lives because of what Jesus accomplished on the cross. In the meantime, while living in this world, we move from trial to trial, being challenged, changed, and transformed by the ups and downs of life.

When I was first saved, I was just a child in the faith. I lacked stability, guidance, accountability, and maturity. I found these things by becoming more consistent and disciplined in my faith and by seeking mentorship. Leaning on others who have been through the same thing helps guide us so that we can navigate the rough terrain of life. Over time, you begin to realize that some of the things that were challenging before are no longer challenging. This happens as you continue to keep your eyes on Jesus, seek godly counsel, and surround yourself with Christlike individuals.

Building Spiritual Muscle

When you exercise a muscle and allow it to rest and recover and then feed yourself nutritional fuel, your muscle gets stronger. Spiritual maturity is like that muscle. When you take care of your spirit by challenging it, disciplining it, feeding it with Scripture, and getting adequate rest, you become more mature. This is different from human maturity. Human maturity is heavily dependent upon age, experience, and time. Just by living, you become more mature, for the most part.

Spiritual maturity, however, is a direct result of your effort. You can be saved for twenty years and still be an infant on your spiritual journey. On the other extreme, you can be saved for one year and be a spiritual elder. It depends on the time, energy, and effort you put into your spiritual growth. Many people who say they're a Christian or a follower of Jesus lack the discipline and consistency to grow and nurture themselves into spiritual juggernauts. When storms arise, they're weak, ill equipped, and easily discouraged.

Two of the keys to advancing your spiritual maturity process are to be consistent and to discipline yourself. You need to show up every day, even when you don't feel like it. Don't allow your emotions to dictate your actions. Make sure you're taking time to rest, to feed yourself spiritual nutrition, to pay attention to what you're consuming, and to monitor your intake of spiritual junk food. As you learn and grow from your failures and mistakes, you should continue to put the time, energy, and effort into the maturity process. You'll see yourself growing in favor and walking in a spiritual authority that many people fail to experience. Most fail to experience this because of a lack of obedience that causes self-imposed limitations.

I was in the fitness industry for years, and many of my clients had specific fitness goals. Some wanted to lose one hundred pounds in one hundred days, others wanted to lose twenty pounds in two weeks, a few wanted to train for fitness competitions, and some planned on adhering to an overly restricted nutritional diet plan. Regardless of what their goal was, they all had one thing in common: excitement! When starting a new challenge, most people are actively inspired and motivated to achieve their goal.

Here's what ended up happening. After a month or so into their fitness journey, that motivation began to fizzle out. Once they got a taste of everyday consistency and discipline, their goals started becoming an inconvenience in their day. I've seen that same excitement and motivation when people start a new one-year Bible plan, when they first join a weekly Bible study group, or when they begin attending church every Sunday. The anticipation of a new challenge typically inspires people, but once those feelings decrease or disappear, they're left shakable and movable, lacking a firm foundation. Sticking to their commitment requires too much work and becomes more than they can handle.

To avoid that outcome, here's what I encourage you to do. Start small. Set goals that are easy to attain without too much extra effort. I believe that success breeds success. When you see yourself doing well, growing, or winning the day without an extraordinary amount of effort, you will gain confidence. By practicing discipline and adding a little bit more to your plate, you will see yourself go the extra mile little by little, day by day. Over a long period of time, that is what truly makes a difference.

I look at sanctification in the same way. God builds us up day by day, battle by battle, victory by victory. The habits we create and build in small ways will help equip us for the large, mountain-sized obstacles that come our way. When we're tired, where do we run? When we're angry, what do we do? Are we quick to pray? Do we rely on Scripture? Do we react out of the flesh? Are we quick to gossip? Are we reflecting and praying before we respond?

It's in those daily habits, those small victories, those minute areas of our lives that we become more like Jesus. We start relying upon the Spirit, and we start surrendering and letting God know that we cannot do it on our own. It is only by His strength, His might, His grace, and His mercy that we are victorious. In those moments when we fail or miss the mark, it's of the utmost importance that we learn and grow from the experience. We don't beat ourselves up or drag ourselves down, and we don't hold it against ourselves. But we are to identify our failures and use them as a springboard to success.

What Is Success?

The world defines success differently from how followers of Jesus define it. The world tells people to chase their dreams, follow their hearts, and use their lives to pursue happiness. If we follow what the world tells us to do, we'll continue the repetitive cycle of getting tossed around. We were put on this earth to pursue a holy and righteous existence that brings glory and honor to Jesus. Culture wants us to believe that the world revolves around us, that we're the center of the universe, and that we are the main character of the story.

That couldn't be further from the truth. True joy, peace, and happiness are found only in pursuing God's plan, purpose, and will for your life. Many people are chasing after the world's idea of success believing it will bring them happiness. But if success, accolades, achievements, and awards were any indication of overall joy, then why do we constantly see successful, rich, and famous people addicted to drugs and alcohol? Why do we observe immorality and relationship problems among that group? Why do we see them choosing suicide at increasingly high rates?

These are signs that the things of this world are worth nothing. The world promises so much yet cannot deliver. The happiness that the world promises is a counterfeit. It looks like it satisfies, but it always falls short. It's only in the plan, purpose, and will for which God created you that you'll find true happiness. That happiness comes from the pursuit of holiness.

When you make Jesus the center of your life, things fall into place. When you have fellowship and a relationship with Jesus and understand that He's the purpose of your existence, you make room for Him to lead and guide you in the direction of your unique calling. The One who made you knows what you were made for and sees you as His child because of the righteousness of Christ. When you start to walk in the fullness of your identity in Christ and are no longer tied to this world, you start to walk differently. The enemy can no longer deceive you, and sin is no longer appealing. You start to despise the same things God dislikes, and you start to look at life through the lens of the Lord. Through that lens, you will see how false the world is.

If you look at a counterfeit one-hundred-dollar bill, you might not be able to see that it's fake at first glance. If, however, you hold it up beside a real one-hundred-dollar bill, you will be able to spot the difference. Where there is an absence of God, the counterfeit seems to truly satisfy.

There are counterfeits everywhere we look, especially when we look through the lens of social media. Nowadays, we can see people's highlighted lives at the click of a button. Many people showcase their successes and achievements but leave out the truth of what is going on behind the scenes. We don't see the struggles, arguments, violence, deaths, financial issues, mental health concerns, and other real-life turmoil and suffering that people experience. Most keep their real, raw, and vulnerable moments hidden. They only present the portion of their life others will deem successful and happy. This breeds a false sense of truth. When we're going through a hard season, we start comparing our reality to other people's great success and achievements. We start to feel as if we're missing something or that they're doing something to make God love them more. We've all been guilty of this.

When you start to live your life for God, you receive a true sense of peace, comfort, and happiness that the world will never understand. Your life might not seem luxurious or successful in the eyes of the world, but you have the ultimate success because you have eternal life in Heaven. The things of this world are temporary, not eternal. In order to fully surrender your life to Jesus, you must turn from the worldly goals you've set and submit to the plan and purpose God has for you. You'll find true happiness by pursuing holiness.

If you're not sure what the plan and purpose is that God has for you, know that it's sharing the Word of God to this counterfeit world so they, too, can accept Jesus Christ as their Lord and Savior and have access to eternal life in Heaven, just like you.

Your True Identity

Because of the death, burial, and resurrection of Jesus Christ, we're now seen as the perfection and righteousness of Jesus. This is good news! Our sin that once separated us from God has been bound up and thrown in the sea of forgetfulness. Our past, present, and future sins have been forgiven. So now we have the boldness and authority to go before God with our prayers, requests, and supplications. We have restored fellowship and relationship with the Creator of the universe.

Our heavenly Father knows us intimately. He created and molded us in our mother's womb, and He wants us to walk in the fullness of who He made us to be. We are no longer our past and no longer our mistakes. We put on a new identity when we put our faith in Jesus. We must remind ourselves of who we are according to Scripture and not who the world says we are. "For he chose us in him before the creation of the world to be holy and blameless in his sight. In love he predestined us for adoption to sonship through Jesus Christ, in accordance with his pleasure and will" (Ephesians 1:4–5).

Too often we allow the world to tell us what beauty is, what success is, what it means to be a man or a woman, or to define us as a person. We've essentially lost our identity. Our identity is in Jesus. The Bible says that we are more than conquerors, that the power in us is greater than the power in this world, that we're a royal priesthood, that we're chosen and set aside, that we're victors and not victims, and that we're children of God.

When you start to see yourself the way God sees you, you start to look at life differently. You start to see your obstacles as challenges that lead to your opportunities. You start to see your problems as platforms to bring God praise. You turn your worry into worship and your fears into faith. You start to speak with boldness because you understand who you are. Most importantly, however, you understand *whose* you are. God's not asking you to be perfect, but He's asking you to trust in His Son who was.

Nothing will be accomplished by your own strength, might, or endurance. It's because of the finished work at the cross and because of the death, burial, and resurrection of Jesus Christ that you have been saved, sanctified, and filled with the Holy Spirit. It is now your privilege to live your life in service to God.

This is the benefit of having a pure heart. "Blessed are the pure in heart, for they will see God" (Matthew 5:8). As you have a pure heart, He will be with you if you make a mistake. He will never leave you, and He will never forsake you (see Deuteronomy 31:6). He will never turn His back on you. Our loving Father will hold your hand and direct you through life until you breathe your final breath and are ushered into eternity.

There's a saying I like to use: "progress over perfection." If there are moments when you beat yourself up for a mistake you've made, remind yourself that we all fall short of the glory of God, and the goal isn't to be perfect, but to make progress. The progress of trying every day to glorify Jesus' name. I look to Philippians 3:13–14, which says:

> Brothers and sisters, I do not consider myself yet to have taken hold of it. But one thing I do: Forgetting what is behind and straining toward what is ahead, I press on toward the goal to win the prize for which God has called me heavenward in Christ Jesus.

Following Jesus is a lifelong process. On your journey with Christ, you will have failures and mess ups, and you're going to be put in situations where you might not always be victorious. This is a constant reminder that we cannot do this on our own. We need to be fully reliant on the Lord, always focusing on what's ahead.

God understands our frailty. He's not caught off guard or surprised when we make mistakes in our weak moments. This is why we need to always draw near to Him, make time for Him consistently, and be in continual fellowship with Him. Don't give up on God and your faith when times get hard, because He will never give up on you. When you mess up, repent from your sin, find an accountability partner, pray, and ask God to help you learn and grow from it and help you change your ways. Remind yourself you might not be where you want to be, but you're further along in your journey than you were yesterday. Continue to pick up the cross every day, die to your flesh, and walk with Jesus.

PRAYER FOR A PURE HEART

Heavenly Father, search my heart. Fill me with Your light and bring to the surface anything that You want me to pay attention to. Lord, I have fallen short, made mistakes, and missed the mark over and over in my life. Help me to see the lessons, to grow, and to mature in those areas. I know that I'm not defined by my past and that You see me as the perfection and righteousness of Jesus. Help me to see myself as You see me. I pray for protection over my mind that I would be aware of the tactics of the enemy who looks to condemn, deceive, and accuse me. Help me to stand on Your truth so that my heart is not jilted side to side by the ever-changing currents of my circumstances. In Jesus' name, Amen.

APPLICATION

1. When have you experienced true repentance? What did that look like for you?
2. To what degree do you believe you're living the life God has created you to live? In what areas of your life are you settling? What's keeping you stuck? Fear, unbelief, worry?
3. What areas in your life need reflection, repentance and progress?

SIX

Exchanging Offense for Forgiveness and Unity

It was hard growing up without a father, but it was even harder being raised by a drug-addicted mother. Her only concerns were her drug affairs, which often left me to fend for myself. I didn't understand how a mother could repeatedly choose drugs over her own flesh and blood. To me, having one parent who was half present and only concerned with her own desires was the same as having no parents at all. My mom's actions and behaviors got her in trouble multiple times. She was unfit to parent me, and because of this, I was placed in foster care. I endured the consequences of her decisions.

My upbringing and difficult relationship with my mom could have caused major mental and emotional damage—if I had held on to the past, my trauma, and our conflict. Before fully healing and forgiving her, I harbored some deeply rooted resentment and unforgiveness. I had to process why she chose drugs over me, why I was sent to foster care, and why I had no parental protection as a child. I felt I had been given such an unfair life.

Those mixed emotions built unstable anger. Throughout my teenage years, that unforgiveness hurt me and hindered my growth. I didn't know God at that time, so I couldn't see how He was moving in those situations. For years, I allowed unforgiveness to harden my heart and get in the way of a healthy relationship with my mom.

It took lots of therapy, personal growth, prayer, and learning how to have empathy for my sister in Christ before I had a better understanding of my mom's issues that led her to choose the lifestyle she did. When I became a parent in my late teenage years, I was able to empathize more with my mother and understand her experience and perspective. I was able to look at life through a different lens, and I started to see beauty in her story. I also saw how God had always protected the both of us.

I stopped playing the victim card. Holding on to the hurt, pain, and trauma kept me from fully understanding and experiencing what God was trying to show me. He was trying to reveal a message to me in the midst of that pain and hurt. I needed to experience those feelings and emotions so that I could redirect my focus onto Him and His greater good for my life.

After you've accepted Jesus Christ as your Lord and Savior, you must work on healing your offended heart. The danger of living with an offended heart is that you're not walking in the fullness of God's purpose for you, which is loving and caring for others. "For if you forgive other people when they sin against you, your heavenly Father will also forgive you. But if you do not forgive others their sins, your Father will not forgive your sins" (Matthew 6:14–15). This is a great teaching to apply to your life.

What Jesus did on the cross caused all of our iniquity and sin to be forgiven. The debt that we accrued was completely wiped away. This was done not because of anything we did or anything that we deserved. His actions were done out of love. We are quick to get our feelings hurt by others and hold on to minor infractions. If we want to be an effective witness and true ambassador of Jesus, we have to be slow to anger and quick to forgive.

When your heart holds on to resentment, offense, anger, and wrongs done against you, you become guarded. You're quick to shut things down with other people when you see indications of red flags. This is what unhealed people do. You're not able to enter the fullness of an open, honest, vulnerable, and transparent friendship or relationship with others. You're holding on to past situations and keeping count of wrongs because you're not fully healed. Building and having relationships with people is an important part of our walk with Christ. Keeping to ourselves and not establishing healthy relationships with people defeats the purpose of having fellowship and community.

You weren't saved to sit on the sidelines and pursue a life of mediocrity. You and I were saved to make Jesus' name more known. We do that through relationships. We do that by interacting with others and showing them the light and love of Jesus. You can't do that with an unforgiving and offended heart. When times get hard or confrontations arise with others, you have to be prepared to communicate in love and truth and not get offended. You can't end the conversation because it's too much for you to handle. If you interact with people, there will be confrontation. People are like sandpaper. They can be abrasive and rub you the wrong way. If you're constantly living life with your walls up and holding on to every wrong done to you, you will start to avoid people. That is counterproductive.

No More Hard Hearts

I'm reminded of the story found in the book of Exodus when God allowed the pharaoh of Egypt to have a heart of stone even after witnessing all the signs, miracles, and wonders that Moses performed (see Exodus 8:15). God sent Moses to Egypt to deliver the Israelites from captivity. God brought very precise and controlled chaos to Egypt so that the pharaoh would release the Israelites. The pharaoh promised to release the Israelites if the plagues God sent to Egypt would stop, but as soon as the chaos and destruction stopped, he returned to his stubborn ways. After he got what he wanted, he did not follow through with his promise of letting the Israelites go.

I believe there are Christians, followers of Jesus, who do the same thing. This is what I like to call "crisis faith." When they're in the middle of a bind or find themselves with their back against the wall, they start begging God to intervene. They hope He will grant their desires, like a genie. They'll make promises to God and make false commitments. As soon as they get what they want, they quickly return to the previous state to which they promised God they wouldn't return.

We tend to do this with forgiveness. We tell God that we will forgive someone, but when the slightest inconvenience arises, or a replay of what we went through crosses our mind, we let that seed of frustration cause us to jump right back into where God delivered us from.

The pharaoh finally gave in and let Moses take the Israelites out of the land of Egypt (see Exodus 12:31–32). Unfortunately, the pharaoh's hardened heart led to his own destruction. As God led Moses and the children of Israel out of Egypt, He took them through the parted waves of the Red Sea to escape. Pharaoh could have left things alone, but he didn't. He gathered his army and followed the Israelites to get them back. His heart had become so hardened that he didn't remember why he was mad or why he wanted to keep the children of Israel enslaved. In pursuit of his own anger, as he and his army were chasing the Israelites through the parted Rea Sea waters, God closed the waves on the pharaoh and his army, drowning them all. But the Israelites made it through safely.

Holding on to things, having a hardened heart, and being led by feelings and emotions only leads to destruction. "I will give you a new heart and put a new spirit in you; I will remove from you your heart of stone and give you a heart of flesh" (Ezekiel 36:26). When we put our faith in Jesus, we invite the Holy Spirit to dwell inside of us. In doing so, we exchange our old, hardened heart for a tender, loving heart made in the image of Jesus, separating us from being ruled by fear, insecurity, worry, confusion, anger, and jealousy. Now we are led by love, joy, peace, patience, goodness, kindness, gentleness, and self-control (see Galatians 5:22–23).

If we remind ourselves whose we are by constantly coming back to the Holy Spirit, we will find that we have no place for unforgiveness. The very essence of God is rooted in mercy, love, and grace. There is no correlation or common ground without forgiveness.

Forgiveness is a challenging topic because many people have suffered real trauma at the hands of other people: betrayal, backstabbing, lies, physical abuse, unacceptable interactions, and other unimaginable things many of us can't even wrap our minds around. When talking about forgiveness, we need to have a clear understanding that when we forgive someone, that does not mean we have to have a relationship with them afterward.

Forgiveness of others is between you and God. Though you can rebuild a relationship with someone afterward, it's not a requirement of forgiveness. You can absolutely forgive somebody from a distance, especially if it's for your mental, emotional, or physical safety. It's important that you set healthy boundaries with those who hurt you when communicating your stance and position. Remember, forgiveness is a choice and something that is done in your heart.

Forgiveness Doesn't Always Mean Reconciliation

My parents' relationship was built around drugs, abuse, manipulation, and pain. I'm a product of their drug affairs. Other than for a short season, my father was not a part of my life. He was around for the first few months of my life, but it wasn't to help raise me. He stuck around because he needed a place to live. From what I was told, when I was three months old, my dad beat my mom within an inch of her life.

When she recovered, she packed everything up and fled to California to get away from him. It became just the two of us. From then until the age of eleven, I only heard stories about my dad—I never met him. Even while living in California, my mom didn't change her environment. She ended up relapsing. She put me on a Greyhound bus, by myself, to Portland, Oregon, to live with my uncle so that she could enroll in a rehab center.

Shortly after arriving in Oregon, my uncle thought it would be best for me to develop a relationship with my dad. After locating him, my uncle took me to meet my dad for the first time. Again, I was only eleven years old. Since that was the first time I had met him or experienced him as a father, I wasn't able to formulate my own opinion about him. A couple months after I met him, my mom finished rehab and came to Oregon to get me.

To my surprise, my mom and dad rekindled their relationship. As an eleven-year-old, this was confusing. I was both concerned and excited that my estranged, previously toxic parents were exploring a restored relationship. I began to imagine a fairy-tale ending, picturing a completed family. But the things that are not in God's will cannot last. After less than a month together, they picked up the old habits and routines from a decade before.

During this time, my mom was working at a senior living facility. She snuck my father and me into the facility basement so that we had a place to stay. With no shower, toilet, or running water, we used a five-gallon bucket as a toilet and washed our hands using bottled water. When we got hungry, Mom would sneak food down from the kitchen. After receiving a week's worth of pay, she would rent a hotel room for the weekend so that we could take a shower and clean our clothes.

My mom's overall goal was to save enough money to rent an apartment for us. She started saving cash in a box. One day, my dad found that stash of money, took it, and disappeared. He left my mom and me in the basement of the senior living home with no money and no way to find him. I watched my mom lose her mind. I was heartbroken, not just for her but for the fact that my dad was gone again. That was the last time I saw him.

How could a father do that to his son? How could he just walk out? How could he lie and betray us? How could he take all our money? I held on to that anger and bitterness for years. It was embedded so deeply that it altered the course of my actions as a teenager. I become emotionless and detached myself from people. I was easily triggered. I didn't care if my actions and behaviors affected or damaged others.

Years later, by the grace of God, I found a way to forgive my dad. I forgave him for leaving us stranded, for how he treated my mom and me, and for not being the father I needed. I forgave him from a distance, meaning I wholeheartedly forgave him, but we no longer speak. Remember, unforgiveness hinders your walk with God. You have to let it go. You have to truly forgive that person who hurt you, regardless of what you went through. Then and only then will you be able to discern if you can forgive and reconcile, or if you can forgive and put it to rest.

One of the greatest parts of becoming spiritually mature in Christ is understanding that all things happen for the glory of God. What the enemy means for evil, God can use for His glory (see Genesis 50:20). He is always in control. Everything has the potential to be a learning experience if we allow it to be. It is not your job to enact revenge, to find your own retribution, or to right wrongs. We stand on the Word of God, which says, "Do not take revenge, my dear friends, but leave room for God's wrath, for it is written: 'It is mine to avenge; I will repay,' says the Lord" (Romans 12:19).

God knows who hurt you, He knows who lied to you, and He knows who abused or traumatized you. Let God handle the injustices in your life. Everything is in God's hands, not yours. These are not your battles to fight. They are His, and the battle is already won. Because of this, we can let go and let God handle every aspect of our lives. We don't have the capacity to handle it all, but He does.

There is purpose behind the pain we go through, and faith means believing there is light on the opposite side. Surrender and seek God's face through all things. God makes miracles out of messes. That is the beauty of serving the Sovereign God, Creator of the universe. Holding on to the past and carrying all the hurt and pain with you is counterproductive. You can't carry all that baggage and still be a useful vessel for the Lord. God is trying to take you somewhere and do something with you, but what you're holding on to can stop you from fulfilling your calling.

Anchors and Guardrails

When you truly know yourself, you're able to implement change in your life. What has worked for me is knowing my triggers, knowing what sets me off, and knowing what hurts me so that I can guard against those things. When we identify the things that send us in a downhill direction, we can put guardrails in place to make sure we don't go those directions. Street guardrails are installed in places where there is a likelihood or a propensity for cars to lose control or veer outside the boundaries. They're put in place to ensure our safety.

In the same way, setting effective guardrails in our life is a necessary practice if we want to be an effective witness for Christ. Knowing how we operate helps us to set healthy boundaries that will keep us from reacting and responding to things that don't represent Jesus. We should remind ourselves that we are ambassadors of Jesus, the salt of the earth, and the light of the world. How we behave and treat other people no longer just represents us, but it also represents Jesus.

Here's what I know. Non-believers aren't reading the Bible. As a believer, I'm the Bible that non-believers are reading. They don't turn to Scripture passages to learn what Jesus said or how He reacted to things; instead, they watch how Christians, followers of Jesus, handle things. They pay close attention to how we react, how we respond, and how we treat others. It's important that our lives are producing the fruit of the Holy Spirit and not the fruit of the flesh. Be alert, be watchful, and try to avoid situations that lead you down the wrong path.

What is an anchor used for? An anchor is used to keep boats steady in one place so they don't drift with the river currents or ocean tides. In a similar way, God is the anchor of our soul. He keeps us grounded when the storms of life try to knock us back and forth. When God is our anchor, He keeps us from being swept away, and we remain immovable. The Word of God is the anchor of our hearts. If we allow the truth of Scripture to anchor us, then storms and tribulations won't be able to deceive us or move us.

We can be easily shaken if we're consumed by feelings of unforgiveness, by unresolved issues, and by past trauma. If the things of this world are anchoring you down, God can't move you forward to where He's trying to take you. Instead of God being the anchor of your soul, you allow the enemy to distract you and put your feelings before the truth of His Word.

Picture this: You and God are on a ship. God hoists the anchor back up, ready for you to start piloting your ship in a new direction. He grabs the steering wheel, leading you on the path you're supposed to go. Suddenly, you drop seven anchors back into the water, causing the ship to stop. Each anchor represents an aspect of your life. One anchor represents your trauma, one anchor represents unforgiveness of a former relationship, one anchor represents past failures, one anchor represents your hardened heart, one anchor represents your guilt, one anchor represents your pain, and one anchor represents your resentment.

You're no longer going in the direction God is trying to take you because you're stuck and you won't let go of the things that have offended you. You have to let God break every chain to those anchors so that your ship can continue to sail and so that God can use you as a vessel for His works. If you don't let Him break those chains, you'll hinder your growth and your journey. In other words, let go and give those hurts to God to dispose of. That baggage can't go where God is taking you. You can't bring things with you that weigh you down. You must focus on what's ahead. Paul says:

> Brothers and sisters, I do not consider myself yet to have taken hold of it. But one thing I do: Forgetting what is behind

and straining toward what is ahead, I press on toward the goal to win the prize for which God has called me heavenward in Christ Jesus. All of us, then, who are mature should take such a view of things. And if on some point you think differently, that too God will make clear to you.

Philippians 3:13–15

Why do we insist on holding on to things that are inconsequential to our eternal salvation? Why do we hold on to grudges, offenses, unforgiveness, and wrongdoings? Who is it truly hurting? Who is it slowing down? Is it the people who hurt us, or ourselves? I want to encourage you that if you want to run this race of life well and walk in the fullness of who God called you to be, you're going to have to let things go. You're going to have to give God full control. You're going to have to lighten the load by laying all those burdens down at the foot of the cross. Keep your eyes on the prize—eternal salvation.

When spiteful feelings rise inside of you toward someone who hurt you, traumatized you, or abandoned you, those feelings can linger in your mind and in your heart. They can be overpowering and can become an idol in your life. These are issues you need to address, not ignore. Surrender those feelings and emotions to God. He will give you the strength to forgive and move forward even when the hurt seems too great. When you pray and communicate with God about your pain, He is listening. He already is aware of how much disruption those hard times have caused you. We have the privilege of being able to give our sorrow to God, and He will heal us and make us whole again.

Prayer is God's way of communicating with you and bringing you comfort. Prayer is where you will find healing, transformation, and answers. It's an absolute honor and privilege to be able to speak to the One who created you. He wants to take all your pain away. The Lord tells us that forgiveness is possible.

When we heal from our unresolved issues, we're able to forgive. When we forgive, we find freedom, because we're no longer shackled by our fleshly emotions. When that happens, we're able to move away from the illusion that we will be able to change the past. That will create in us an open heart so that God can use us as His willing and able vessels. Remember, with every person we forgive, we're paving the way for the next time we forgive. We grow stronger, gain more courage, and learn to invite God into the process sooner.

PRAYER FOR FORGIVENESS

Father God, help me to let go of any past hurts, traumas, or unresolved issues onto which I may be grasping. Help me to seek reconciliation and forgiveness. I know that You have extended grace and mercy to me, not holding my offenses over my head. Help me to extend the same mercy and grace to those who have sinned against me. I know that unforgiveness is like a poison to my body, so heal me. Reveal to me anything that I might be holding on to unknowingly. I know it's easy for me to overlook sin that I've held so close to my heart. I want to let it all go. I surrender. I no longer have the capacity to hold on to wrong things done to me. I lay it all down at the foot of Your throne, and I look to You to help lighten my load. Thank You for always forgiving and protecting me. I love You. In Jesus' name, Amen.

APPLICATION

1. How has unforgiveness been a hindrance in your relationship with God? How has unforgiveness been a hindrance in your relationship with other people?
2. What things are you holding on to or are having a hard time forgiving? What do you need to let go of?
3. What steps can you take to initiate healing in your relationships where there are unresolved issues?

SEVEN

Eliminating Distractions to Find Consistency

Social media is one of the largest distractions we face today. As of a latest poll, there are 4.59 billion people worldwide who use social media, which is about 58 percent of the global population.[1] It's increasing every day. Social media can be both a blessing and a curse. When it's used wisely, it can reach millions of people around the world. I believe social media will become one of the primary outlets that will help us fulfill the Great Commission, which urges us to preach the Gospel in all corners of the earth (see Matthew 28:19).

People download social apps to connect with other people across the globe, but the algorithms that social media platforms implement pull people further from truth. As people showcase their lavish and worldly lifestyles, we begin to

1. Maryam Mohsin, "10 Social Media Statistics You Need to Know in 2022," *Oberlo.com*, https://www.oberlo.com/blog/social-media-marketing-statistics.

compare our lifestyle with theirs. People are seeking attention, fame, and rewards. Those who don't stand firm in their
foundation with Christ start submitting to the things of this
world based on the perception of worldly success. We're
quick to believe that someone's social posts reflect their
daily reality. We see images of attractive families, adventur-
ous trips, upscale homes, luxury cars, perfect body images,
skilled talents, trophies, accolades, and healthy lifestyles. It
leaves us to assume everything is perfect behind the scenes.

Here's the reality. What people post is curated content.
Many won't post their daily struggles, their low moments,
the obstacles they face, or any real-life problems they're facing. They reserve their losses for behind closed doors. When
you pair these superficial, surface-level lifestyles with the
oversexualization of society, you have a ticking time bomb
in your hand. If given free rein, social media will pull at
your attention, take your focus off God, and consume all
your free time.

It is my observation that people are on social media three
to six hours a day. Think about it. What do you do when
you're waiting in a line? What do you do when you're going
to the restroom? What's the first thing you do when you wake
up? What's the last thing you do before you go to bed? What
do you do on your lunch break? What do you do when you're
relaxing on the couch? We've normalized our moments of
free time to opening our phones and checking our social
media feeds. It has become more of a way to escape our
current reality than a way to connect with others.

We used to gather all the news and information from the
local newspaper and television news stations. We weren't
bombarded with news unless we were reading the paper or

had tuned into the news channel. Today, no matter which social media platform you're on, news headlines are everywhere. Whether that's someone voicing their opinion on the latest event, reposts of a news article, or the platform itself advertising a particular story, we see the updated world news in a matter of seconds. These resources are constantly updated with events happening all around the world. If you spend a lot of time on social media, the world as we know it is expiring right before our eyes. Everything seems to be falling apart.

Based on the headlines, you start believing the enemy is gaining victory. This is contrary to what the Bible says. From Scripture, we know that God has everything under control, even in the midst of what we see as chaos. The messages we receive are not only overwhelming, but they're also false. We are bombarded with information, and it is distracting us from the plan and purpose God has for us. If the enemy can get you to be more concerned about culture than God's Kingdom, how will you ever fulfill your calling? We must look past all the distractions, open our hearts, and remember that God is in control and knows what He's doing.

Redeeming Social Media

Part of my daily life is creating Christian content for social media. The platform I have belongs solely to the Lord. He has given me the gift of being relatable and approachable so that the Gospel can reach His people through me. I don't take this calling lightly. I strive to stand strong in my faith, values, and foundation in Christ. As a social media content creator, I often spend four to six hours a day editing and posting content, responding to comments, and answering direct messages strictly for spreading the Gospel. Today I'm very disciplined when using my social media, but that wasn't always the case.

When I first joined social media platforms, I was easily distracted by worldly content. I went down rabbit holes looking for information, and I got lost in mindless scrolling. I'll never get that time back! The more time I spent on social media, the more I compared myself to other content creators in my niche. I measured my success against my peers, or I found my worth and value in the performance of my posts. I allowed my feelings and emotions to rise or fall based on the popularity of what I was doing. It was an emotional roller coaster and was damaging to my self-worth. I allowed the opinions of commenters to affect me, and I often spiraled into moments of depression and sadness. This took a toll on my mental health.

After hitting a point when I wanted to throw in the towel and leave social media, I prayed and asked God for guidance, provision, and direction. I knew my calling was to preach the Good News of Jesus, but the distractions were causing me to doubt myself. As I cut out all distractions and spent alone time in His presence, I was able to hear Him when He spoke to me. Through prayer, He reminded me that I was made for such a time as this. He revealed to me that with the right guardrails, boundaries, and blueprint, I could use social media in a healthy way. I could use it in a way in which it has an eternal impact and adds value to people's lives without causing me to get distracted or being a burden in my life.

As I started implementing barriers and blocking the things that were pulling my attention away from Him, I was able to establish a healthy relationship with social media. I no longer found my identity, value, or worth in my performance. I got confirmation directly from God instead of seeking validation from people. I allowed God to use me as a vessel for the Holy Spirit in my posts, and I let my posts reach those God intended to reach regardless of how many likes or comments the posts received. When I completely surrendered my time, energy, and effort, God gave me more territory to cover, and He stewarded higher levels of performance for His glory. This is how social media can be a blessing and not a curse.

A Sound Mind and Heart

How do I keep a calm mind and heart in all the chaos and distractions this world offers? By remaining in constant prayer and having a daily commitment to reading the truth of God's Word. This is where our firm foundation is found. When it comes to reading the Bible, we've gotten comfortable with consuming the context without thought or comprehension. We read the Bible as a spiritual duty instead of viewing it as quality time set aside for us and God.

The idea of setting aside spiritual devotion time can seem boring, laborious, and somewhat exhausting. That devotion time starts feeling more like an obligation you have versus embracing the privilege you have to speak with God and spend time in His presence. It's like when Jesus was in the Garden of Gethsemane. After He came back from praying and speaking with the Father, He found the disciples sleeping. Jesus told them, "You men could not stay awake with me for one hour?" (Matthew 26:40 NCV). This speaks volumes!

Can we stay awake? Can we stay in tune with the Holy Spirit? Can we stay focused on God for an hour of our day?

The reason prayer is an essential ingredient for our lives is because when we have open, honest, and vulnerable conversations with our Father, we're able to take inventory of the active things in our life. This helps us to identify what's a distraction or what's pulling us away from God. If your mind starts to wander in a different direction while you're praying, be intentional and catch yourself. Your distractions could be caused by things such as work, your phone, obligations, or other commitments. You may also be future tripping, which involves worrying and obsessing over the what-ifs. I suggest leaving your phone in another room, turning off the episodes playing in your head, then finding a quiet place where you can get alone with God. Don't allow your prayer life to take the back seat when it needs to be your driver.

Here are four things I've done to not just establish a strong and vibrant prayer life but to produce a sound heart and mind. These things have given me divine direction to my thoughts, behaviors, and emotions, allowing me to have a more intimate connection with God. I believe that consistency is the bridge that takes you from where you are to where you want to be. Many people lack consistency in their prayer life because it becomes challenging. People allow their feelings and emotions to dictate their actions. When it comes to actually seeing results in any area of your life, you have to find a flow of consistency and discipline.

1. Audit Your Time

There were a couple areas in my life in which I had to audit and prune. The first thing I had to audit was the time

I spent on social media. Not only did I audit the time spent, but I identified and unfollowed social media accounts that caused me to get distracted or that could lead me astray, pruning the branches that weren't bearing fruit (see John 15:2). The second thing I had to audit was the time I spent with people who left me feeling drained, tired, or overwhelmed. Sometimes the lack of motivation from the people in our close circle can limit our focus as to where God is calling us. This doesn't mean we have to cut them out of our lives completely, but we must be mindful about auditing our time with them. It can be easy to overlook the time we're spending with people who are hindering our growth, so be alert.

2. Establish a Routine

One of the greatest practices that has helped me eliminate distractions is creating a routine and sticking to it. We should implement discipline in the areas that pull at our attention. We should limit those things that take priority over our relationship with Jesus. When I was in the fitness industry, I would often ask my clients what they thought the best diet plan was. They would give straightforward answers like the Zone, Atkins, Keto, Paleo, or whatever the current trending diet was. My response was simple: the best diet out there is the one that you will do consistently. Once you give up on the plan, schedule, and routine, you lose the ability to see true results. We get excited to start a new challenge, but as soon as it becomes an inconvenience or a struggle to keep up with, we throw in the towel. When it comes to your prayer life, it's all about setting yourself up for success.

3. Create a Schedule for Prayer

Commit to praying at the same times every day, maybe before bed, when you wake up, on your lunch hour, when you pick your kids up from school, or all the above. Set alarms on your phone or put sticky notes in places that will help trigger that reminder. It isn't that we only pray during our scheduled times, but having a schedule helps create a structured prayer system. We don't want to forget to talk with our Creator each day. In addition, make it a spiritual practice to pray in the moment that you see or think about people instead of gossiping about them. Fill yourself with constant communication with the Lord.

4. Show Up Regardless of Feelings

Get into the habit of sticking with your prayers, even if they seem repetitive. You may have experienced a season in your life when you feel that you are praying for the same old things or for the same people. You might begin feeling it's unnecessary to pray as much because you have already said multiple prayers for the same topic. If you're believing for a prayer to be answered, no matter how long it takes and no matter how many times you've prayed over it, you need to stay in discernment and communication with the Lord. He can hear from you what your heart desires. As you stay in full submission to His will, you will receive a pure heart. He's working on answering your prayer, whether His answer is yes, no, not right now, or a redirection of what you should be praying for. God isn't trapped by time. You can't limit Him. What you pray for today may be answered years down the road. The same goes for people who continue to pray for you. You may experience an answered prayer that someone prayed over you a long time ago that they never gave up praying.

We shouldn't take praying to our Father lightly. He is the only One who helps refine us, shape us, and give us strength. When we audit our time, establish a prayer routine, and show up—regardless of our feelings—we start to value the connection we have with God. When we stay consistent in prayer, the enemy becomes nervous because he's not able to use our surroundings to discourage, disappoint, and distract us. When we have a sound mind and heart, the enemy can no longer disrupt our life.

Gaining Clarity and Consistency in Prayer

When we understand that the enemy is after our soul and he doesn't want us to have a relationship with God, we gain clarity. This helps us to remove distractions. God wants to speak to us, and He does so in a number of ways. Though God can speak to us very loudly and clearly, what I've experienced the most are His whispers. In order for us to hear a whisper, we have to get close. God's not going to yell over the idols we've exalted to get our attention. He's not going to yell over the things that are pulling at our attention. He's not going to yell over the loud obstacles we're facing. God is a gentleman. He's not going to force us to spend time with Him. He wants us to choose Him, to seek His face, to seek His love, and to follow His direction.

Imagine walking into a crowded room where everyone is competing with each another to speak and share their stories. Someone starts projecting his or her voice louder to be heard over the talking crowd, then the next person starts speaking louder, and so forth. It becomes a yelling match as everyone tries to be heard. You're now in the noisiest room, filled with the distraction of people waving their arms and hands around as they speak.

While you're talking with someone in this crowd, you look over and see someone in the corner all alone smiling at you. He does not take his eyes off you. He motions with his hand for you to come over and sit with him. This is how our Father is with us. There's an empty seat right next to Him that He has saved for you. He wants you to sit and talk with Him, but He's not going to yell or put on a show to get your attention.

God is constantly sending us invitations to spend time with Him. Will you choose Him, or will you continue your conversation with the world? God is sitting in the chamber of your heart, desiring relationship and fellowship with you. He wants you to choose to sit with Him. Lots of things are competing for your attention, but He wants you to make Him a priority. When you deeply desire a relationship with God, nothing will stand in your way. If you're not making time for Him, it's because you've allowed the things of this world to become more important than the Creator of the universe.

When there's an abundance of noise, there's a lack of peace. One verse that helps keep me focused is, "You will keep him in perfect peace, whose mind is stayed on You, because he trusts in You" (Isaiah 26:3 NKJV). This is a reminder to always come back to God. There will forever be distractions and things pulling for your attention. It's up to you to be conscious of your environment and be aware of what those things are.

Consistency comes with reflection, prayer, auditing, and taking inventory. We need to implement a regular checkup in our lives to see where we're spending our time, where we're spending our money, and how we're using our resources. Even when we're focused on the Lord, it's important to do a heart posture check-in because many times our environment can subtly change without us being aware. Based on our circumstances, we can become distracted and out of focus. If we get too comfortable and let things interfere with our schedule, we will stop having daily fellowship with God.

When a professional photographer is about to take a photo, he or she focuses the lens on the subject so that it appears crystal clear. If the subject starts moving, the photographer must refocus the lens so that the subject becomes clear again. In a similar manner, we need to keep our eyes on God when He's moving in different directions in our life. We must constantly refocus and stay in alignment with Him. We can't lose focus!

When you start to walk in consistency, you will see situations change, and you will see results. This breeds confidence. It's invigorating, encouraging, and uplifting. When you start reading your Bible consistently, things start to make sense, your eyes are opened, and the Holy Spirit starts to lead you and guide you in ways that you never thought possible. When you start praying and spending time with God on a regular basis, you become aware of how He's moving in your life. You realize when He redirects you and when He speaks to you. Because you've built a deeper connection with Him, you know Him in a more intimate way.

As you develop a relationship with another person and spend more time with them, you start to notice things about them that other people may not notice. You learn new things about who they are, what makes them happy, what makes them sad, and what interests you have in common. I've studied my wife so well and have spent so much time with her that if we're at an event and someone makes her feel uncomfortable, I can tell by her body language, a raised eyebrow, her facial expression, or even the tone of her voice. The amount of time we've spent together helps me to know her in such an intimate way that she can speak to me from across the room without ever saying a word. This is the beauty of time spent together consistently and without distraction.

God desires an intimate relationship with you that goes far deeper than any earthly relationship could. When you enter a deeper relationship with God, He speaks to you, not just through the Word of God or the confirmation of the Holy Spirit, but through people, music, art, nature, and in many other indescribable ways. The foundation of this beneficial relationship starts with consistency, showing up, and spending time with Him.

PRAYER FOR CONSISTENCY

God in Heaven, I know that I can make all the plans in the world, but You establish my steps. I'm thankful for the breath that You breathe into my lungs, so help me to use each one wisely. I understand that time on this earth is limited, so help me to steward it well. I ask that You help me rid myself of any distraction that is pulling my attention off You. Fix my eyes on Jesus. I know that You are the same yesterday, today, and forever. Help me to see the freedom that comes with consistency and discipline. I don't want to become rigid and religious, but I want to honor each day that I have the privilege of living. Teach me to honor the opportunity. In Jesus' name, Amen.

APPLICATION

1. What things are currently distracting you and pulling at your attention?

2. Create an ideal prayer schedule for your day. It's not something that has to be rigid or set in stone, but having an outline of what a solid day would look like for you is extremely helpful.

3. Execute the schedule. Put the plan into action. Do your best to adhere to the plan and take notes of what went well and what didn't. After reflecting and auditing, do it again. Create a revised schedule based on your experience. Then do it again. Rinse and repeat. Do this for the week until you find a good, consistent routine.

EIGHT

Repairing Relationships to Create Peace and Accord

God designed us to have relationships with our brothers and sisters in Christ. One of the unfortunate consequences that came from the Fall of man is the broken relationships that occur because of our selfishness, stubbornness, and self-centered attitudes. Hurt and broken relationships are inevitable. Did you ever have a best friend with whom you no longer have contact because of a fallout, gossip, or relational drama? Did you have a parent who was in and out of your life as you grew up, or who was not present at all? Did your first love break your heart? From a young age, we become familiar with broken relationships. Many of those relationships were never repaired, and we had to move on from them.

What typically happens when we move on from an unresolved or unrepaired relationship is that we develop defense mechanisms, behavioral patterns, wrong assumptions, or unhealthy expectations. These are all relational preconceived notions we add to the baggage we carry from relationship to relationship. When we don't take the time to heal, address the issues, and grow from these expired relationships, we project our negative experiences from previous relationships onto new ones. Because the door of our past hurts and traumas is still open, we tend to put up walls to avoid the same negative feelings we've once experienced before. It is important, therefore, to allow God to repair your heart, restore your faith, and help you to build new, healthy relationships that are founded on the rock of Christ. He wants to help you close the door to any broken relationship in your past and begin new Christlike relationships.

For you to successfully move forward in life, you need to accept that there's a healing process you must undergo because of old, broken relationships. Part of the healing process is forgiveness. Many of us want to move forward, but the weight of our pain keeps us from being where God wants to take us. It's almost as if we're tied to our emotional damage, becoming stuck and unable to prosper. God wants you to cut ties with those emotions. He can't take you to the next level or to the next season of your life until you have released what you're holding on to. You can't fulfill all your spiritual duties in the Kingdom of God when you're wrapped up in old things.

Here's how I look at it. There's a very narrow door you go through to get to the next season of your life. You must allow God to whittle away the rough edges of your character and allow Him to shape and mold you just right so that you can fit through that door. You can't run through the door because you won't fit. You can't break down the door because it belongs to God, and you're not strong enough to do so without Him. You can't bypass the process of healing. So, it comes down to a decision. Do you go through the repairing process of being shaped and molded for the next season, or do you remain the same and endure the pain of consistently getting the same results that lack purpose, direction, and fulfillment?

As I've gone through season after season, I've had to allow God to shape me into the newness He's called me to be. I've had to forgive, release, and heal from the past in order to move forward. There have been relationships that I've had to repair, people I've had to forgive, others I've had to ask to forgive me, and relationships I've had to let go of and let God handle without carrying baggage from it.

My mother and I didn't develop a strong, repaired relationship until a few years ago. While we've always been in communication, we've lacked a fulfilling mother-son relationship. I remember the moment we had a deep, heartfelt conversation that we both desperately needed. A few years ago, I brought my three sons over to her house to visit, and we stayed the night.

That night, we were all in the living room watching a movie. I remember feeling the Holy Spirit nudge me to talk with her about how I felt growing up under her care. At first, I just ignored it. We all know that feeling. I didn't want to talk, and I didn't want to go that deep with her. I didn't want to explore our past or talk about that old life. I just wanted to watch the movie. She ended up pausing the movie to grab a snack, and upon her return, the Holy Spirit spoke to me very loudly saying, "Now!"

As she sat down in her chair, I said, "Can we talk?"

She responded, "Of course, son."

I began to ask her questions about her upbringing, wanting to know what it was like. This opened a conversation I never thought I needed, but God knew I did. It put so much into perspective. Because of that conversation, I had a completely different view of who she was. I felt so much empathy toward her. She had been a woman who had made many sacrifices and mistakes, but she had still tried. I had a better understanding of what she had gone through as a child, where her heart posture was when I was a child, what her mindset was at that time, and why she did the things she did.

My mother is a child of God, and He had His hands on her the whole time. She, too, experienced His love, mercy, and grace. He has filled her with the Holy Spirit and has given her an amazing testimony of the transformational love and power of the blood of Jesus Christ. When I looked at her story through the lens of Jesus and not the lens of this world, I began to love her as my sister in Christ. Three hours and many tears later, we had created a repaired mother-son relationship that had been damaged for over twenty years. After this, I felt free and new. That night, not only did I experience a release of childhood baggage, but I healed from a hurt that I didn't realize I was holding on to. I felt free to love my kids deeper, and I felt covered by the love of God.

This moment was a perfectly orchestrated event God had me experience so that He could refine me, shape me, and prepare me. Now remember, it was the nudging of the Holy Spirit that I didn't ignore that helped create peace in my life.

Think about all the times the Holy Spirit has nudged you to do something, say something, initiate a conversation, or reach out to somebody—and you've ignored it. When that nudge makes us feel uncomfortable or seems inconvenient, it's easier for us to ignore it. Are we trying to move forward, but unresolved issues, broken relationships, and the past are keeping us stuck right where we are?

Three Tools for Better Relationships

Your relationship with God sets the tone for what your relationships with people will look like. Your most important relationship is your relationship with God. If there is dysfunction or an issue in your relationship with Him, then all other relationships in your life will follow suit. There are three relational areas we need to focus on with God that will improve and strengthen the relationships we have with people. These tools will create more peace, unity, and fulfillment in our lives.

1. Communication

This is arguably one of the most foundational elements of any healthy relationship. Most marriage counselors will say that good communication between couples leads to a more connected marriage. When we've learned how to better communicate with God, we end up having better communication with people. If you find it hard or challenging to pray to Him, you're going to find it challenging to communicate with people. If there is dysfunction in your communication skills with the One who gave His life for you, knowing all your mistakes and failures, you're going to have dysfunctional communication skills with people who don't know all your mistakes and failures.

Talking with God not only establishes your relationship with Him, but it also sets the precedent for communication in all relationships you build. If I don't take time to communicate with my wife, then we won't be in unity. I will no longer understand her. I won't know what she wants, where she's going, or how she feels about things. Staying in alignment with her becomes a challenge. In the same way, communicating with God through prayer creates harmony, recognition, and alignment. That's not to say that you will always be clear on what it is that God wants or where He's going, but through prayer and Scripture, you'll always know how He feels about things, and you will be able to live accordingly.

2. Understanding

The second relationship area to focus on is truly understanding the other person. It's so important that I know my wife, who she is, what she likes, where she wants to eat, how to engage with her, when she likes to go to bed, what's her favorite vacation spot, and when I need to give her space. There's value in knowing what she wants from me, where she sees our marriage going, how we're going to raise our children, and how we're going to be partners in this life. As her husband, it is my responsibility and privilege to learn all about her and to stay curious and passionate about who she is. She is God's gift to me, so I want to take care of this relationship.

In the same way, it is our privilege to know God, who He is, what He wants, how He operates, what He expects from us, and how we are to live in a way that honors and glorifies Him. We get to know God on a deeper, more intimate level by reading His Holy Scripture. It's not just a history book. It's a love letter He has left us that is filled with direction, guidance, wisdom, knowledge, correction, His desires, and everything we need to know about Him.

Many Christians say they can't hear from God, yet these are the same individuals who keep their Bibles closed. Reading Scripture shouldn't be a chore or a burden. When you're in relationship with God and realize that the primary way He speaks to us is through the Word, you start to hunger and thirst for it. The desire to know Him better and to hear His voice pushes you to the Bible. When you have questions and need answers, you run to His Word for wisdom and understanding. The Bible has the greatest impact on your life and helps develop spiritual maturity.

3. Quality Time

Spending quality time with God without distractions is a monumental focal point to your earthly relationships. If you can spend quality time with the Lord without distractions, you'll find it easier to spend quality time with the ones you love without worldly distractions. Valuing the precious time that you spend with our Father creates peace, unity, and fulfillment within all the other relationships you have.

When I make time for my wife, I put my phone down, I engage in conversation, I look her in the eyes, and I focus solely on her. Our relationship thrives the more we spend one-on-one intimate moments together in which we both feel seen and heard. Our time is our most precious commodity.

To spend your time with another person, knowing you can't get that time back, is one of the most loving and meaningful gestures you can make.

That's why spending uninterrupted time with God is filled with intimacy. It's one of the most life-changing practices you can implement. If you're allowing worldly distractions to stop you from spending time with Jesus, you're going to end up allowing the world to distract you from spending quality time with those you love. Our healthy relationships with others are modeled from our healthy relationship with God.

As we take time to communicate with God, get to know Him on a deeper level, and spend quality time with Him, we see the importance of these three areas in the context of relationships with people. If you look back on any friendship or relationship you've had, you can take accountability that you could have done better in one of these categories. We've all experienced the loss of a relationship. There is purpose behind every relationship you have had, even if that person is no longer in your life. When you ask God to reveal the purpose of that relationship, He will unfold the lesson. You might have been a lesson for them, or they were a lesson for you—or both.

Some of these lessons were hard and painful. Some were filled with love and fulfillment. Some were shorter, and some were longer. In whatever way they were expressed, relationships don't lack meaning. Relationships help build our character and inspire growth for new relationships. If you apply these three tools to strengthen your relationship with God, you will see how much better your relationships with other people become.

Your Most Important Relationships

Having a firm foundation in Christ provides peace and comfort, knowing that you can call on Him when you need help repairing a relationship or moving on from a relationship. Ask God for guidance, provision, and direction in the next steps of healing as the magnitude of relational hurt varies. To better protect your heart and to remain in full alignment with God's will, ask Him to close doors that aren't from Him. Pay close attention when He's giving you signs that He's closing the door in a relationship. There are many doors and opportunities that are not from Him, and these can cause distraction, discouragement, frustration, heartache, and disappointment.

The brothers and sisters God brings into your life are given so that you have fellowship and so that you don't have to do life alone. Make sure you're surrounded by like-minded individuals who don't lead you astray. You have a unique relationship with each person, but it's of the utmost importance that we remain in unity and in one accord in each relationship, especially those who have direct access to us and who are an integral part of our lives.

> Make every effort to keep the unity of the Spirit through the bond of peace. There is one body and one Spirit, just as you were called to one hope when you were called; one Lord, one faith, one baptism; one God and Father of all, who is over all and through all and in all.
>
> Ephesians 4:3–6

The Body of Christ is not supported by one person. It's supported by all of us because we are stronger when we work together; therefore, we have to be in unity with our spouse, in unity with our parents, in unity at church, and in unity with our brothers and sisters in Christ. These are the most important relationships we can have, as they protect our walk with Christ.

When we face the weapons that form against us as one accord, the Spirit creates an impenetrable circle filled with prayerful and intentional warriors of God that cannot be moved. "Where two or three are gathered together in My name, I am there in the midst of them" (Matthew 18:20 NKJV). When we come together and pray, not only do we feel supported by family, but we experience God's presence. That further advances our growth, worth, and development as a believer. Don't be nervous about stepping up and coming alongside another brother or sister and praying for them. And don't hesitate to ask another brother or sister to pray for you. God doesn't want you doing life alone.

PRAYER FOR HEALING

Heavenly Father, I don't want to carry any baggage through the doors that You're opening for me. Help me to surrender and lay down anything that I might be holding on to. I pray that if there are any broken relationships in my life that You wish to restore, You would show me what they are and help healing come. I pray that if there is any dream, vision, or goal that You want to breathe life into, You would resuscitate it. I only want to go where You're calling me. Help me to be in alignment with Your plan, purpose, and will for my life. Help me to walk in a manner that is healthy and whole. I want the freedom that comes with following Jesus, so help me to unpack my baggage that is filled with the issues I've been carrying. My life is in Your hands. Have Your way with me. In Jesus' name, Amen.

APPLICATION

1. In what relationships has communication been an issue? How often do you struggle to understand others or feel as though you're misunderstood? Why do you think that is?

2. What broken relationships do you feel led to repair? What unfinished business or unmet goals need to be revisited? Not all relationships need to be reconciled, but is God highlighting any in your life? Make a list.

3. How can you take steps to reconcile those relationships and restore unity? Ask yourself this question: Is this from God or my own desire to be in one accord?

NINE

Establishing Healthy Physical, Mental, and Emotional Habits

During the summer between my freshman and sophomore year in high school, a friend of my mom's offered to let me, my half brother, and my mom move into his house as he had extra bedrooms. For financial reasons, my mom couldn't pass up the offer. The house was a three-story historic building with a very beautiful backyard. It had an old-fashioned, colonial architecture look, and it was a very classic home. We were more than happy to stay there because we had never lived in a house before, especially one as beautiful as this. As soon as we moved in, my mom and brother got comfortable. Dealing with unhealthy coping mechanisms, I couldn't allow myself to get comfortable. By this age, I'd learned that as soon as I got comfortable, something bad was going to happen.

Not to my surprise, something unfortunate did happen. It was about mid-summer when my mom got in trouble. Not only did she have past warrants, but she'd committed a handful of new crimes, and she was taken to jail with no date of release. The police were informed she had two children, so they came to our new home and removed both my brother and me. They handed us each a bag to fill with as many clothes as we could fit inside. That's all we were allowed to take.

When we got to the police station, a representative from Child Protective Services told us we had to go into foster care until further notice. My half brother's dad was notified, and he immediately traveled from Nevada to Oregon to pick my brother up. I, however, didn't have anyone for them to notify. My brother and I were separated when he went to live with his dad in Nevada. I stayed in foster care until my mom completed her jail sentence, which was about one year. During that year, I finished my sophomore year of high school. Though this event was traumatic at the time, it led to a lot of maturity and transformation in my life.

While in foster care, I adopted new habits and routines. I allowed myself to feel comfortable and safe because there was now stability and a solid foundation in my life. I didn't have to worry about where I was moving to next, what I was going to eat, or whether or not my mom was doing something she shouldn't.

Being in foster care was where I developed discipline and consistent character traits. I had structure in my life, which is something I had never experienced. Before going into foster care, I had never liked school. I had horrible study habits, I was rebellious, I smoked a lot of weed, I drank alcohol, and I was very mischievous. Getting attention for being a troubled kid was better than no attention at all.

Despite my best efforts to sabotage my time in foster care, my foster mom was persistent, patient, and firm. If I wanted something, I had to work for it. If I wanted to go somewhere, I had to ask for permission. My foster mom requested a detailed plan of what I was doing, when I was doing it, where I was going, and what time I'd be back. If our timeline didn't line up, there were consequences and lost privileges. I learned there were systems in place, and if I transgressed against them, it disrupted my life. If I played by the rules, I had a lot more freedom and got to do more things I enjoyed.

I established an after-school routine to balance home-work, chores, and playing basketball. By completing all my assignments, attending school every day, and establishing a good routine, I finished my sophomore year with a 4.0 GPA. That was a huge accomplishment for me, and it built confidence in myself. Not only did I have an opportunity to be a kid and thrive, but I also learned that when I applied rules, regulations, routine, and order to my life, I could be successful at anything.

As the school year ended, I started to prepare for a fun and eventful summer in my foster care home. I made plans to play sports and join my friends in summer activities. One week into summer break, my foster mom received a call that they were releasing my mom and she would be picking me up. Although she was clean, sober, and had completed all her required classes to get me back, I didn't want to go with her. To be honest, I was scared that I would lose everything I'd worked so hard to gain. My future looked bright, my new friends were good influences on me, my environment was stable, and I had structure. Unfortunately, children in foster care don't have a voice, so I was placed back into my mom's care.

I left foster care with a new understanding of how to be consistent and disciplined. When I applied these two traits in all aspects of my life, they yielded the results I wanted for my future. I learned how to operate successfully within boundaries and guidelines. That year in foster care planted seeds of development that would be unlocked later in my life.

The Importance of Consistency and Self-Discipline

Consistency and discipline are two nonnegotiable traits we need to cultivate in our physical, mental, and emotional habits to be successful. Many people rely on either motivation from others or external motivation to inspire them to establish good habits, but that won't keep them going. Relying on outside sources won't sustain success in the long haul.

Let's say external motivation is the spark that ignites the fire to your success. While it might get the fire started, having self-discipline and consistency are the only things that will keep your fire burning, leading to long-term success. The small daily habits we form and repeat over a long period of time keep us from burning out, and they yield consistent results. If you want to increase the size of your fire or alter the results of your success, bigger consistent habits will equal bigger results. Motivation and inspiration don't keep the flame going; they merely help get it started.

This is the same motivation and inspiration people get when starting a physical health journey. They get fired up, ready to begin their journey to a healthier version of themselves. But shortly after, they find it hard to keep the same motivation they had in the beginning. This is when consistency and discipline must be applied. To achieve and maintain physical health goals, they have to implement a routine and stick to it. They must have self-control and an unchanging agreement with themselves.

Although we can't dictate our external circumstances, we can control what we eat, the way we move, how much we rest, and the way we hydrate ourselves. The choices and decisions we make within our control can alter our physical health. If we lack discipline and self-control, we're not taking care of God's temple.

Our body houses the Holy Spirit. "Do you not know that you are God's temple and that God's Spirit dwells in you?" (1 Corinthians 3:16 ESV). Since the Holy Spirit dwells in you, it's important that you keep His house clean and in order. When you take care of your physical body, you become a more effective vessel for the Lord. You can also nurture the body God gave you by praying over it. Stay in constant prayer over your health, your body, your mind, and your heart.

Another area we often overlook is our mental health. We might ignore the severity of our hostile thoughts or believe the doctor when he or she tells us there is nothing to worry about. Not only should we pray over our mind, but we need to adhere to habits that benefit and heal our mental health. If we don't, our thoughts will hold us captive in a little box, torturing us. As things start to accumulate in your mind, the weight of it all starts building a stronghold on you. Taking mental breaks is essential to healthy living. When you take a mental break, you're detaching from distractions and worries, and you are forcing yourself to shut everything off and find something that brings you joy.

Whether it's running, reading, making art, crafting, taking a long bath, getting a massage, or lying in bed with calm music playing, we receive benefit from anything that slows our mind down. If you need to, ask for help so that you can take time for yourself. We all need alone time, a break from the kids, a day away, help in the house, a therapy session with a professional, or help at work with our overwhelming projects.

You can't do it all, and you can't carry the weight of everyone else. God knows you're not capable of handling everything. Only He is capable of handling it all, which is why we give it all to Him. "My grace is sufficient for you, for my power is made perfect in weakness" (2 Corinthians 12:9). When you acknowledge this, you start throwing away some of those abrasive thoughts.

Another way to protect your mind is by detaching yourself from worldly things. Worshiping idols, obsessively comparing yourself with others, and caring too much about what other people think of you will produce insecurities and feelings of worthlessness and failure. When you restrict what your eyes see, you can control what your heart desires. This facilitates a healthier mind and protects your thoughts. As you stay in constant prayer with Jesus, ask for a renewed mind and that chains will be broken. He has the authority to heal you in a moment's notice.

I have personally experienced God's transformational love and healing from mental health issues. Not only did I seek healing from our Healer, but I also supported my healing journey by completing therapy sessions, seeking godly counsel, reflecting on my past, and addressing all of my issues head-on. There is no shame in seeking professional help. There are many godly counselors who can help you navigate the process of healing your thoughts.

Do not ignore your mental health, especially if you feel that seeking professional help is a sign of weakness or that you don't have enough faith in God to be healed. The truth is that many of us come from dysfunctional homes. As we emerge into adulthood, we carry the residue of unresolved childhood trauma and emotional damage. Many of us lack the tools, skills, and resources to properly cope, process, and grow. Many Christians struggle with mental health issues and don't even know it. Most of us, if not all of us, would benefit from seeking help from a faith-based professional.

The Bible tells us, "Where there is no guidance, a people falls, but in an abundance of counselors there is safety" (Proverbs 11:14 ESV). Stay consistent in seeking counsel from our heavenly Father and seek godly wisdom from your brother and sisters in Christ. That includes professional counselors. Establishing healthy mental habits is essential to having a healthy walk with Christ.

In the same way, having healthy emotional habits are just as essential to having a healthy relationship with God. Due to the lack of awareness of our mental health, we often lack the skills and the personal development needed to handle the emotional aspects of life. Many believers are led by their feelings, living day by day on an emotional roller coaster. Their emotions lack a foundation. They don't have the ability to face hard problems that arise. Grief, tragedy, discouragement, heartbreak, and failure will happen to all of us. How we react to them emotionally is a choice and should be Christlike. When we experience emotionally difficult events, we must make good decisions around what we can control, and we should trust God with the rest.

This is how we create healthy emotional habits. The more we make good decisions, stay consistent, and remain disciplined, the more we create healthy patterns in our minds. Our goal is to handle difficult experiences how Jesus would handle them.

Regardless of the pain and hurt you experience, your emotional response is one hundred percent within your control. If you frequently allow your feelings to lead you—instead of letting the Holy Spirit lead you—you need to refine, develop, and repair that area of your life. That's not to say that you can't share your raw emotions with God through prayer. In fact, that's the exact authentic relationship He wants with you. God wants that transparent and vulnerable relationship with you because He knows just how healthy that is for you to fully trust Him with your feelings. It's when you stop sharing your feelings and emotions with Him and start allowing them to dictate your actions and behaviors that you need to complete a heart-posture check. To do this, ask yourself some conviction questions. Is my behavior a reaction to my feeling of being hurt, betrayed, or disappointed? If yes, devote some time with God to seek restoration. Did I perform this action because I allowed my fleshly response to get the best of me? If yes, readjust your character to fit Jesus' character. Apologize to God, to yourself, and to others involved, not just for your spiritual healing, but to teach yourself how to apply healthy emotional habits.

Building Intimacy with God

One of my favorite characters in the Bible is King David. When I read about his relationship with God, I realize that I can approach God with honest pain and still feel safe. The book of Psalms paints a picture of a man who shared his honest, vulnerable, and raw emotions with Him. No feelings were off-limits. David went through life experiences that led him on an emotional roller coaster of despair, self-pity, loneliness, and abandonment. Yet even during his darkest times, through prayer, observation, and realization, he always returned to his faith in the Lord. He adopted healthy habits that redirected his thinking to reflect trust in God. He remembered everything God had carried him through.

Regardless of the highs and lows, David navigated through his emotions by talking to God about his concerns, affections, and environment. David had so much confidence in God based on his past experiences. He knew God would carry him through any situation. He learned how to cope with emotions that included worry, doubt, and fear by fully surrendering them to God.

After evaluating the reality of his situation and allowing himself to express the resulting emotions, David consistently returned to the truth of who God is and what God said about David. There's something special about recalling all the battles God has won, all the victories through which God has carried you, all the storms that He has quieted, all the valleys He has led you through, all darkness

He has illuminated, and all the weapons He did not allow to prosper.

David knew God because he spent time with Him. He was obedient to the Holy Spirit dwelling in him, he counted all his blessings, and he knew God's heart—because he pursued it. This is the kind of relationship I strive to have with God every day. It's up to me to develop my relationship with God in a way that goes deeper than just reciting a prayer, giving Him a wish list of my wants, or aimlessly making empty promises to get out of situations. It takes effort and intentionality to build a strong bond with our Father.

When you focus on applying consistency and discipline in your physical, mental, and emotional health, you start to strengthen your relationship with God. This is paramount in the life of a believer. If there is dysfunction in one of these three areas, there will be dysfunction in your spiritual walk. Though you'll never have perfectly healthy habits or have everything figured out, if you continue to work hard in these areas of your life, you will develop stronger tools.

Do not check out or give up simply because you're not seeing results immediately. Working on your physical, mental, and emotional health is a lifestyle and a lifelong journey. We constantly have to circle back, check in, reevaluate, and be intentional about our health.

God is an intentional God. Let's be intentional about our relationship with Him. To be intentional means showing up deliberately. It's not always easy. Some days are harder than others, and you won't always feel like applying these practices. But if you show up, you won't regret it. If you schedule a workout session, show up. If you set up an appointment for therapy, don't cancel it. If you plan alone time to calm your mind, don't fill it with distractions.

When you set your mind on something, draw up a monthly game plan, execute it, and watch transformation happen. Remind yourself that at one point you saw the need, and you made a choice to address it. Showing up means following through with the commitment you made to yourself and to God.

This world tells us to find balance in all things. Spend time with friends and family, find a job where you only work so many hours, find time to go on trips, find time to spend with God, find time to work on your mental health, and find time to go to the gym. So many things are pulling at our time and attention, and we're supposed to find balance in it all.

I don't encourage you to seek balance. I encourage you to seek guidance from God on what He wants you to do. As you continue to apply structure and routine to your day, remember that when it comes to balancing your day-to-day life and your spiritual walk with God, one far outweighs the other. Your salvation and eternal life do not hold the same weight as the things that are temporary. Your prayer life, devotion to reading His Word, spending time with Him, and worshiping Him carries more weight. "Seek first his kingdom and his righteousness, and all these things will be given to you as well" (Matthew 6:33).

As you put God first and focus your attention on knowing Him, He will lead and guide you in the other areas of your life. The closer you are to Him, the clearer His plan becomes for you. If you're truly walking with God in the fullness of what is available to you, your life will be filled with reflection, adjustments, revelation, and development.

PRAYER OVER MY BODY, MIND AND SOUL

Heavenly Father, help me to be more intentional with how I spend my time. Help me to take the steps necessary to take care of the temple You've put me in charge of. Help me to prune and audit the areas in my life that have become out of balance. I pray that You would touch my mind with Your peace that transcends all understanding and that You would put me around people who will help me create a healthy environment. Lord, I'm tired of being complacent and settling for less than what You have for me. I pray that You would ignite a fire deep inside my bones that gets me headed in the direction that You've called me. Have Your way with me. My heart and my soul are Yours. In Jesus' name, Amen.

APPLICATION

1. To what key areas of your life do you need to apply discipline and consistency? What are steps you can take today to implement some changes? How can you enlist the help of another person to hold you accountable in some of these areas?

2. Do you feel that professional help could be beneficial for you? If so, have you ever sought godly counseling? Would you be open to it? If you have, what were your thoughts about it?

3. How has your church helped or hindered you in these areas? Are you an active part of a church that you

attend regularly, or are you in between? If you're not in church, what's keeping you away? What steps can you take today to get connected to community and fellowship?

4. Is your life out of balance? If so, what steps can you take today to restore balance?

TEN

Allowing the Holy Spirit to Speak When You Don't Have the Words

When God first started providing opportunities for me to speak and share the Gospel onstage, I would write out these elaborate speeches. They were filled with detailed notes, bullet points, and biblical references. My goal was to execute the speech with precision. Instead of using discernment and making sure the Holy Spirit was speaking through me, I found myself speaking based off my notes that the Holy Spirit had me prepare.

While you may believe that's the same process, it's not. Following an outline that's filled with the Holy Spirit is merely using a conduit for information to teach on. Allowing the Holy Spirit to speak through me allows room for God to speak, transform, and move mountains. For that first year of speaking engagements, I only followed my outlines and didn't leave space for the Holy Spirit to move.

As I remained in constant prayer with God, I asked Him to use me and speak through me. Over time, I started to notice that what I wrote down was not what was coming out of my mouth. I found myself following only the bullet points the Holy Spirit had me write down.

As my discernment has grown stronger, I've concluded that when I empty myself and allow the Holy Spirit to fill me with His words—whether I have the words to speak or not—He speaks through me with life-changing wisdom. God knows who needs to hear something and when they need to hear it. I'm merely a vessel for the Holy Spirit. It's up to me to allow the Holy Spirit to work in and through me. If God will use someone like me, a person who was once lost, angry, and broken, then He'll use you, too.

I had a mentor who gave me some profound godly wisdom. He said, "If you're not allowing the Holy Spirit to work through you, you're getting in the way of what God wants to say." It was the confirmation of what I had been feeling: I needed to let go of my notes and trust the Holy Spirit. Preparing for a sermon by making notes is part of the process, but it's crucial that we pay close attention to the leading and nudging of the Holy Spirit. If God is leading the lesson in a different direction, I must honor that.

A part of my flesh felt that this freedom was unorganized. I worried that if I didn't adhere to my notes, I might say something that didn't make sense, or I might stumble over my words. I didn't want to say something that was heretical or that contradicted the Bible. But we aren't called to worry about our performance; we are called to trust in Him.

I had to break my fleshly thinking habits, empty myself of my concerns, and fill myself with Him so that He could do what He does best.

Learning to lean on the Holy Spirit and not let my insecurities get in the way took some time, but I had to learn fast because God was moving very quickly in my life. There wasn't time for me to worry about myself. He had many places and spaces to take me to spread the Gospel. This is why we die to ourselves daily, pick up our cross, and follow Him.

Looking back, I can recall the exact event I spoke at that officially broke the seal and set me free from my preaching insecurities. I had written an elaborate and meticulous set of notes with multiple elements I wanted to share with that particular audience. On the day of the event, I could feel the tangible, heavy presence of the Holy Spirit. I felt a sense of burden, like I was going to get in the way of something incredible. I felt as if there was a weight on my shoulders that needed to be released, and my mentor's words kept replaying in my head. As I listened to the first guest speaker who opened the event, the Holy Spirit told me to save the notes I had prepared for another time. I was to follow His lead that night. His voice was loud and clear.

This wasn't a surprise to me, as I knew God had been working on me as a preacher and believer. I knew to listen and follow Him. When I went onstage, I gave a brief introduction about who I was. Then to open my message, I looked down at my notes, looked back up at the crowd, and reluctantly informed them of what was going on. I told them I had an entire message written out, but God wanted to do something different.

I closed my notepad, shared a brief, yet powerful word the Holy Spirit wanted me to share, and asked those who wanted to accept Jesus Christ as their Lord and Savior to come to the front. Dozens of people chose to follow Jesus that day. Other church leaders stood up, laid their hands on those who had responded, and prayed an earth-shaking prayer over their lives. This urgent altar call was not in my playbook, but it was in God's. As His vessel, I followed His lead.

From that beautiful moment forward, the way I prepare to preach the Gospel looks different. I'm more concerned with emptying myself of me and creating a space that God can fill. I want to preach in a way that's led by the Holy Spirit, by prayer, and with devotion to Scripture. I prepare sermons by getting into the presence of God for days, sometimes weeks in advance to eliminate all distractions. I allow myself to hear what God is going to speak. I write bullet points down more as a reference—not a checklist or outline. During my message, I allow the Holy Spirit to take the lead. This spiritual strategy works for me. This process has allowed God to do mind-blowing works and to facilitate transformation in people.

Being Led by the Spirit

The same Holy Spirit who dwells in me dwells in you. You can have the same obedience and willingness to allow the Holy Spirit to lead you. You don't have to be a pastor or a preacher to welcome the Holy Spirit to move through you. You don't need a seminary degree for the Holy Spirit to intercede on your behalf.

Even if you aren't confident in your ability to speak the Gospel or don't have all the knowledge from the Bible, you can allow the Holy Spirit to speak on your behalf to your sphere of influence. You can share the Good News of Jesus with a mom at your son's soccer practice. You can be working as a receptionist and share the Gospel with clients in the waiting room. You can be standing in line at the DMV (Department of Motor Vehicles) and strike up a conversation with someone who needs a reminder of how much Jesus cares for them.

In real-time conversations, really listen to what people are sharing with you. Get to know their heart posture and pray that God gives you the words to speak. From there, allow His words to flow. Do not allow the limitations you've put on yourself to stop you from sharing His name. The beauty of the Holy Spirit is that He will give you the words to speak to a particular person or group even when you don't have all the answers. Even if you never share a verse from the Bible, you can still communicate how much Jesus loves people and how important they are to God. You can walk them through accepting Jesus Christ as their Lord and Savior.

Our purpose in life is to spread the Gospel at whatever capacity we're able. If God gives you the ability to spread the Gospel around the world, make sure you follow your calling. If the unique gift God has given you is in music, then worship the Lord and bring others into God's presence with you. If your gift is leading fellowship groups, make sure you step into your calling by discipling those God brings into your groups. Our callings all look different, but our purpose is the same. It is and will always be to spread the Good News of God's Son, Jesus.

In the same way that the Holy Spirit gives you the words to minister to others, the Holy Spirit also gives you the words to speak to God in your personal prayers, even if you don't have the words to communicate. Have you ever started a prayer knowing you need God, but couldn't find the right words to say, or nothing came out when you tried? Scripture says:

> In the same way, the Spirit helps us in our weakness. We do not know what we ought to pray for, but the Spirit himself intercedes for us through wordless groans. And he who searches our hearts knows the mind of the Spirit, because the Spirit intercedes for God's people in accordance with the will of God.
>
> Romans 8:26–27

Sometimes, all you can do is offer a tear as a prayer. In those moments, the Holy Spirit is your mouthpiece, because He bears witness to the purpose for which God created you. He knows exactly what you need. These kinds of moments hit home for me. There have been times in my life when I would attempt to pray but couldn't even form a sentence. I would just look up at the sky and nod my head. In these moments, I know God understood how I was feeling. I know the Holy Spirit is interceding on my behalf. I'm confident that the Lord feels my vulnerable emotions even though they're not verbalized. God desires a real, authentic, and transparent relationship with us. Knowing that the Holy Spirit intercedes on my behalf brings me joy. We don't always have to perform an elaborate or lengthy prayer. He knows what we need even when we can't articulate it.

The Holy Spirit doesn't just intercede on our behalf when it comes to speaking to God and other people. He also dwells in us to protect us from our flesh. "You, however, are not in the flesh but in the Spirit, if in fact the Spirit of God dwells in you. Anyone who does not have the Spirit of Christ does not belong to him" (Romans 8:9 ESV). Because the Holy Spirit dwells in us, we have an inner sense of what is and is not pleasing to God. I believe that when we feel anxious, discouraged, depressed, overwhelmed, or exhausted, the Holy Spirit is alerting us that we are out of alignment, heading in the wrong direction, stagnant in our faith, or drifting away from where God wants us to be.

Because the Holy Spirit dwells in us, we have this navigation system that alerts us when we're off track. Many of us have grown so accustomed to these feelings that we start to label ourselves with mental health issues. Sometimes, all we need is a spiritual correction. Some people will even self-medicate with drugs, alcohol, and prescriptions to quiet that inner voice. In essence, it is the Holy Spirit telling us we're going down the wrong path. Because of this, it is important that we remain intentional with our spiritual development, with growing our spiritual muscle, staying in tune with the Holy Spirit, and taking time to pray and reflect with God about our lifestyle.

When I don't have the words to pray, I read prayers that the Word of God provides. The Bible is my battery, and when my energy is low, I connect myself to the Source that fuels me. It helps jump-start my prayer life. I have written out one of my favorite prayers.

He who dwells in the shelter of the Most High
will abide in the shadow of the Almighty.

I will say to the LORD, "My refuge and my fortress,
    my God, in whom I trust."
For he will deliver you from the snare of the fowler
    and from the deadly pestilence.
He will cover you with his pinions,
    and under his wings you will find refuge;
    his faithfulness is a shield and buckler.
You will not fear the terror of the night,
    nor the arrow that flies by day,
nor the pestilence that stalks in darkness,
    nor the destruction that wastes at noonday.
A thousand may fall at your side,
    ten thousand at your right hand,
    but it will not come near you.
You will only look with your eyes
    and see the recompense of the wicked.
Because you have made the LORD your dwelling
        place—
    the Most High, who is my refuge—
no evil shall be allowed to befall you,
    no plague come near your tent.
For he will command his angels concerning you
    to guard you in all your ways.
On their hands they will bear you up,
    lest you strike your foot against a stone.
You will tread on the lion and the adder;
    the young lion and the serpent you will trample
        underfoot.
"Because he holds fast to me in love, I will deliver him;
    I will protect him, because he knows my name.
When he calls to me, I will answer him;
    I will be with him in trouble;
    I will rescue him and honor him.

With long life I will satisfy him
and show him my salvation."
Psalm 91:1–16 ESV

This Scripture passage helps me take my focus off my inability to put together my own words and place them onto Jesus. This passage is more than just a prayer. It's also a strong weapon that I use to help me when I'm under attack.

The enemy wants nothing more than to distract and confuse you. Have you ever got into prayer and negative thoughts started popping into your mind? *You're wasting your time. God doesn't hear you. You're too far gone.* This happens to a lot of people. One of the ways the enemy tries to pull our focus off Jesus is by bringing our past failures, mistakes, and blunders to mind.

The devil is the accuser of the brethren, and by digging up errors from our past, he keeps our eyes off the present moment and what the Holy Spirit is trying to reveal we need to fix. We can't have our eyes on both the past and present at the same time. God forgave our sins, and the Holy Spirit dwells within us, so every day we must empty ourselves and fill the chambers of our heart with Him.

PRAYER FOR WISDOM AND GUIDANCE

Dear God, I know that You desire an intimate relationship with me. Help me to be more intentional about carving out time to be alone with You. I set aside all distractions and things that pull at my attention. I want to know You better. In the moments when I don't have the words to speak, I know that You see my heart. You know all things about me: my wants, my needs, my dreams, my visions, and all my desires. I want to know what You want for me. As I take a moment of silence to be alone with You, I pray that You would speak to me. Give me ears to hear so that I don't miss what You're saying. In Jesus' name, Amen.

APPLICATION

1. Do you recall a time in which the Holy Spirit interceded for you when you couldn't find the words to speak? How do you interact with the Holy Spirit?

2. What verse can you run to if your prayer life gets stale? Make a list of 3–5 verses that can be a firm foundation to stand on when your prayer life needs some help.

3. Take time today to get still. We are often bombarded with notifications, messages, and people who need us. We don't take time to get quiet. Right now, make room for five minutes of total silence. Shut everything down, close your eyes, be still, and say, "Lord, speak to me." What did God say?

ELEVEN

Quelling Doubts and Questions by Submitting to God's Will

Something I find very challenging is when my dreams and visions don't align with God's will, plan, and purpose for my life. I've had many dreams deferred and many journeys redirected by God because He knows what's best for me. Though His plans for my life are different from my self-seeking plans, one thing is for certain: God's hands of protection have always been on me. If I got everything I wanted instead of God providing me with everything I need, then I wouldn't have a reason to put all my faith in Him.

Many times, the things we want are rooted in fleshly desires. Without us realizing it, those things can become a hindrance, can cause damage, and can be a distraction in our life. They can even pull our attention off God. We can't see the future of where our dreams will take us, but God knows. If we continue to chase dreams that are outside of His will, it will only lead to heartbreak, failure, and disappointment. Jesus will have to come and pick up all our broken pieces.

It's not easy getting to a place where you're able to separate your will from God's will. That in-between space can feel defeating. It can feel as if He doesn't want you to enjoy nice things. That, however, couldn't be further from the truth. God wants the absolute best for you. That's why we have to pray for doors that aren't from Him to close, and doors that are from Him to open. We don't want to walk through any doors that God Himself didn't open. Once we speak with Him, it's our spiritual duty to discern, listen, and submit to His will the first time. We have to learn how to surrender our goals, ideas, and visions and place them at the foot of His throne. We must trust that when He opens and closes doors, it's for our good.

As a father, I pray that my kids become who God has called them to be. I pray they follow the plan and purpose God has for their lives. I want the absolute best for them because of my deep love for them. The decisions I make on their behalf are solely for their protection. If one of my kids wanted ice cream right before bed on a school night, I would tell them no. They would return to their room upset and feel as though I never let them enjoy anything. They don't understand that I know what will happen if they eat ice cream late at night. The large consumption of sugar before bed will keep them up, they won't get good rest, and they won't have full potential to function well in school the next day. Though they may not see it now, one day they will understand why I said no to things, why I said "not right now" at times, and why I redirected their paths when I saw danger up ahead.

In the same way, our heavenly Father knows exactly what we need, why we need it, and how we're going to receive it. When He doesn't answer our prayers according to our expectations, we must realize that His love, mercy, and grace is written all over His answer. God will stop us from running our lives into a brick wall even when we don't understand what is happening. Rejection and redirection are ultimately His protection.

Seeking God's Will and Plan

When I was 23, I had a prophetic word spoken over me. I was told that I had been called to ministry, that I have words of gold, and that I would speak to millions of people about Jesus. When I heard this word, I immediately left the church—that was not part of my dream or vision for my life. My dream was to finish school and become a business owner. This discouraged me so much that I left the church I was attending and went my own way. I went on to earn two college degrees, start my own business, and pursue success in the eyes of the world.

I thought I knew what I needed, so I took full control, ignored God's direction, and forced things to go my way. After accumulating all those achievements, awards, and accolades, I was still heading down an unhealthy path that was outside of God's will. In the end, everything I had worked so hard to build came crashing down. I lost everything I had worked so hard to gain. Here's the thing: I lost everything because I had been focused on building my own kingdom instead of building God's Kingdom. My plans were doomed to fail. The beauty of the Father's love is that even in my rebellion, God was able to use the mess I had made and turn it into a miracle. Even in my disobedience, God was able to use my experience to further prepare me and develop me for His overall purpose.

That time in my life was dark. I was self-seeking, envious, unkind, impatient, and empty. I lacked purpose, there was no peace in my life, and, despite my efforts, I was never satisfied. My spirit was constantly agitated. I was never able to get enough of whatever I was chasing. I was running a marathon with no finish line. The Word of God warns against this in Ecclesiastes 1:14, saying, "I have seen all the things that are done under the sun; all of them are meaningless, a chasing after the wind."

At the end of the day, chasing after money and success, giving in to temptation, achieving the highest levels of success, pursuing everything that this world tells you will bring happiness is a waste of time and is meaningless. It's like chasing wind. You're unable to catch it or contain it. Because I couldn't find happiness in the things that I thought I wanted, I grew numb. I was disconnected and not in alignment with the purpose for which God created me; therefore, there was a constant, internal struggle between what my flesh wanted and God's will.

Now, a decade later, I'm living that prophetic word that was spoken over me, using the words of gold God has given me to spread the Good News of Jesus Christ to millions of people. As always, God's purpose prevailed over my selfish, shortsighted vision of what I thought I wanted. I'm so grateful that it did. I'm now experiencing more heartfelt satisfaction and purpose walking in my calling than I ever felt walking outside of His will.

One of the greatest hindrances we wrestle with is our expectation of how our life should look. The issue of comparison is so prevalent in our culture because we observe what other people are doing on social media. We begin to measure our success against the success of others. This increases expectations in our life.

We create a false set of expectations based on other people's highlight reels, filtered images, and illusions. We want to go places someone else has gone, dress the same way someone else is dressing, speak the same way someone else speaks, or own the same car our neighbor is driving. Our dreams, visions, and goals start to change, and that creates high expectations that may never happen. Because we want what someone else has, we put ourselves in a constant battle with the things of God. When we don't get those things, we start to doubt Him. We find ourselves questioning God's plans for us.

Setting goals for your life isn't necessarily a bad thing. In fact, I highly encourage it. When you set goals, you create direction and a life trajectory. If your goals, however, end up not aligning with His plans for you, then you must be prepared to accept and fully submit to what it is that He wants you to do, what He wants you to have, and where He wants to take you. When you pray and seek His guidance and provision in all that you do, God will lead you. Proverbs 16:9 reminds us, "In their hearts humans plan their course, but the LORD establishes their steps." Even as you prepare a plan for yourself, be ready to surrender it all and get in a posture to understand that God's way is better than your way.

If He changes the directions of your plans, know it's going His way and that's the way you want it to go.

It's Natural to Doubt

Part of being human is wrestling with doubt and struggling to follow God's directions. Don't feel insecure in your faith because you have moments when you struggle to follow His direction. Many of God's children in the Bible struggled with doubt and questioned Him.

God told Jonah to go to Nineveh to let the people there know that God was upset with them, but Jonah didn't want to go. He didn't want to fulfill that specific purpose. In fact, he packed up his things and fled in the exact opposite direction (see Jonah 1:1–3). Since Jonah was traveling on a boat, God orchestrated a storm that caused Jonah to be thrown overboard. Then God sent a whale to come and swallow him. But Jonah didn't die. He sat in the belly of that whale for three days until it vomited him out onto the beach.

Those three days were long enough for Jonah to think about the direction he was going in his life. He had a change of heart (see Jonah 2). Ultimately, he surrendered it all at the feet of God's throne and went where God called him to go.

How many of us can relate to this story? I sat in the belly of a whale for over ten years trying to get my bearings and trajectory straight before I surrendered it all to God.

Another relatable story in the Bible is about doubting Thomas, one of Jesus' twelve disciples (see John 20:24–29). After Jesus' resurrection and transfiguration, Thomas did not believe that He had resurrected from the dead, even though the other disciples told him they had seen Him. Even when

Jesus visited Thomas and stood right before him, Thomas didn't believe right away. He wasn't convinced until he saw the nail holes in Jesus' hands and feet. He had doubts, he had questions, and he needed proof. How many of us have asked God to prove Himself to us?

Then there's Peter, a follower of Jesus who couldn't seem to understand why God needed to give up His Son, Jesus (see Matthew 16:21–23). As Jesus shared God's plans with the disciples of how He would be betrayed, beaten, crucified, and resurrected three days later, Peter had the audacity to pull Jesus aside and start to rebuke God's plan because he did not want these events to happen to Jesus. He didn't understand or want to accept God's bigger plan. But like us, he was looking at the situation from his limited human perspective.

Each of these men had other plans, had doubts and questions, and wanted to be in control. They were human, like us. Wrestling with these things is part of our humanity and part of what we give up when we fully surrender and submit to God. People have turned the word *submission* into something negative. When people hear the word *submit*, they automatically feel defensive. The thought of yielding themselves to a higher authority makes them feel weak.

That's not the case when we submit ourselves to God. God created us to intentionally yield to His knowledge, His commands, His teachings, His wisdom, His guidance, His provision, and His direction. When we yield ourselves to Him, the Most High King who holds all power and authority, we should see that as a sign of love, not weakness.

When we submit ourselves to Him, it shows how much we love Him and are willing to be vessels for His work.

Submitting to God isn't a onetime thing. You have to surrender and submit to God every day by tuning in to the frequency in which God moves. In order to tune in to this frequency, you have to spend quality alone time with God by cutting out all distractions, diving into Scripture, and speaking to Him through prayer. This will help you to hear His voice or feel the Holy Spirit nudge you to go a certain direction, perform a specific action, accept or decline an opportunity, or be in agreement with advice you may have received from a brother or sister in Christ. If you're not tuned in, you might miss the miracle He puts right in front of you.

Let me share an analogy God put on my heart one day when I was at a park. Imagine you're sitting on a bench at a dog park watching people walk their dogs. You start to notice how differently dogs behave. You see that some dogs stop every five feet to sniff a plant or mark their territory. While their owner is trying to direct them, other things pull at the dog's attention. They're easily distracted. The owners have to keep tugging on the leash to get their dog to follow them and continue walking.

Then there are dogs that are practically dragging their owners by the leash. They're running ahead of their master, pulling the leash that's in their owner's hand. Their anticipation of what's ahead can barely be contained.

You also see other dogs that are weaving in and out of their master's legs, tangling themselves with their leashes, and wrapping themselves around trees. They're confused about which direction they should go, even though the leash is an indication of who is in charge of directing them.

There are also dogs across the park that are barking at every little thing happening around them. Their owners have to constantly correct them.

But the dogs that stand out the most are the ones that are walking side by side, in step with their owner. When the owner stops to talk to somebody, the dog sits down patiently and waits for the command to walk again. The dog does not run off, run ahead, get distracted, act disobediently, or bark. His eyes are locked on his owner. When his owner goes left, he goes left. If his owner goes right, he goes right. The dog is aligned with what his master is doing and where the master is going, and he completely trusts the intention of his owner. He is paying close attention to his owner's every move.

When I said we submit to God by tuning in to the frequency in which He moves, this is how tuned in we should be. When your eyes are locked on God, you won't miss the miracle He has for you. While our walk with God is far more intricate than dogs and their owners, this illustration paints a picture of what we look like to God. God sees that we're easily distracted by shiny things, we get ourselves tangled up in situations, we lose focus on what we're doing, we try to run ahead of Him, we ignore His voice, or we constantly complain. We are so worried about the future (our legacy, building an empire, or chasing a world that doesn't care about us) that we miss out on what God is trying to do in our lives currently.

Filled with Purpose

Many people live a life that never fulfills their true purpose because they never submit to God. All that *submitting to God* means is fully trusting Him to guide you and having faith in Him. You have a major role to play in the Body of

Christ. Let go of what you think life is supposed to be and let Him lead you. Life isn't all about you.

God created us to serve Him, and it's an absolute privilege to serve our Creator. That's why many things in our life don't go our way—they're going His way. When you find yourself praying for a specific outcome that never happens, trust that God's will is prevailing in your life. Even the discouraging responses from God have goodness and love written all over them. This tough love can be hard to grasp at times, but the more you rid yourself of you and the more you fill yourself with Him, the more God can work in and through you.

God's will for your life isn't a destination! You will never fully arrive at His perfect will. He wants you to choose Him every day so that He can use you every day. Each day comes with its own set of objectives and is an opportunity for you to walk out the plan and purpose for which God created you. He's not asking you to do a mission trip every day, feed the unhoused community every day, or preach a sermon every day. He's simply asking that you allow Him to lead you each day.

Whether you're taking a day to rest and fill your cup, talking to a friend who needs Jesus, paying for someone's groceries, scheduling an outreach event for an upcoming weekend, attending a weekly Bible study, spending time with your family, or simply being a light in this dark world, commit to following His lead. You are the hands and feet of Jesus. "For we are God's handiwork, created in Christ Jesus to do good works, which God prepared in advance for us to do" (Ephesians 2:10). The fact that God woke you up today is a blessing in and of itself. When you start to steward each day as a blessing that is filled with purpose, you start to see the beauty that's right in front of you.

PRAYER FOR SUBMISSION

God in Heaven, I thank You for hearing my prayers and always answering according to Your will. Help me to have the discernment and understanding to see the goodness in all that You do. I surrender to You all my unmet goals, my doubts, my fears, my worries, and my concerns. I trust that You want what's best for me and that You are working all things out for Your glory and my good. Help me to see Your hand in every season of my life. I trust You, and I proclaim that I want what You want for me. I devote today to walking in step with You. I pray this in the power of Jesus' name, Amen.

APPLICATION

1. What dreams, visions, or goals of yours have not come to pass or have been delayed? How does that affect your faith? How does that change your view of God?

2. What doubts or fears are you struggling with? It's all right to have questions and to wrestle with things. Take time to write them out.

3. What are some prayers you feel God may not have answered?

4. How has God protected you, redirected you, or saved you from a disaster by not doing things your way?

5. Be intentional about trusting God in every aspect of your day. Surrender to the truth that if things are not going your way, they're going His way. That's something to get excited about.

PART III

Discerning Answers to Prayer

TWELVE

Three Important Things to Pray For

There's not just one way to pray. You don't have to approach God with a college degree to get through to Him. He wants you to come as you are and to speak to Him as though He's your Friend and your Father. God wants us to come boldly, without fear of judgment, and pour our hearts out to Him. Usually our prayers look different depending on who we're praying for, what we're praying for, and what season we're in. We have the absolute privilege of being able to talk to the Creator of the universe whenever we desire, and that's exactly what He wants from us. Share what's on your heart with Him. Ask Him to intervene in your life when things aren't going right. Lay all your dirty laundry on the table. Go to Him for protection and provision. He's your Friend and Father who wants to be involved in every aspect of your life.

The more you speak with God, the more mature your prayer life becomes. As it matures, you start to sharpen your discernment. As you get closer with Him, you realize that He already knows all your problems, what you need, what's hurting you, and how He's going to help. If you trust that God knows what He's doing, then you can start talking to Him about the solution. Pray and ask for things to be done according to His will, not yours.

Although we often focus on asking God to answer specific requests and intervene in particular ways, I don't believe that's how we should approach Him with our situations. In fact, I believe there are three very important things we should ask for in prayer that will strengthen our connection with God, will change the scope of how we view the things we're praying for, and will help ensure that we're following God's will, plan, and purpose for our life.

Seek Knowledge

The first thing you should be praying for is knowledge. We want to be made aware of facts and information through reading the Bible and our personal experience. The Bible says, "For the LORD gives wisdom; from his mouth come knowledge and understanding" (Proverbs 2:6). As I walk with God, I'm in constant prayer, asking Him to reveal things to me through His Word. I want the Author of my life to teach me and show me what's not seen by the untrained eye. I want God to download specific skills and qualifications to me that are not only acquired by experience but can be downloaded supernaturally. What I've found over time and through personal experience is that if I ask God for knowledge instead of giving Him a list of my needs, my view of the situation changes.

There was a time in my life when all I did was ask God for financial breakthroughs. As I spiritually matured, I learned different prayer tactics. I changed the way I prayed and started asking God to give me knowledge about finances. With this new prayer strategy, my outlook on finances and money started to change. God gave me divine insight on how to analyze my savings and ways to be more disciplined in my finances, and He highlighted areas in which I needed to prune or audit my spending habits.

Rather than asking God for a financial miracle every time I came up short, I started asking for the knowledge to manage the finances He's given me. Many times, it wasn't my lack of money, it was my lack of knowledge on how to steward the money that I already had. God was providing more than enough to meet my needs, but because I lacked self-discipline and knowledge, I felt a financial burden that was self-perpetuated. Proverbs reminds us that, "An intelligent heart acquires knowledge, and the ear of the wise seeks knowledge" (18:15 ESV).

My prayers are now, "Lord, give me the knowledge to see my situation differently, and give me the experience and skills I need to be a better steward of my finances." You can apply this approach to any situation you face. Praying for knowledge in each situation you experience is an essential tool to remaining on the path God has you on. Your faith can't easily be altered as you now bear wisdom.

Uncover Understanding

The second thing you should be praying for is understanding. To *understand* means to grasp or comprehend the meaning of something. God is always speaking to us, whether it's through His Word, through worship music, through other people, through an image, through our dreams, or through nature. It's important to ask God to reveal anything He needs you to understand so that you don't miss what He's trying to tell you, and you most certainly don't want to misunderstand what He's asking you to do. "Trust in the LORD with all your heart and lean not on your own understanding; in all your ways submit to him, and he will make your paths straight" (Proverbs 3:5–6).

You don't want to lean on your own understanding of how to handle situations. God doesn't want to just provide us with knowledge; He wants to provide us with the ability to comprehend His teachings and His directions. He wants us to speak His language so that we can follow His lead. When we don't pray for understanding, we can sometimes miss the message or instruction He puts right in front of us.

We can find ourselves misunderstanding Him even more when we don't want to hear what He has to say because it doesn't align with our expectations. Not every opportunity is from God, so it's important we identify the things that are from Him. That knowledge comes from God granting you understanding. Let's say you're in a frustrating or challenging season right now. God has you there because He needs to refine and prepare you for where He wants to take you; however, because it's hard or makes you feel uncomfortable, you start taking control to relieve the pressure. If you're not asking God for understanding during this time, you'll only see this season or situation as an attack from the enemy instead of viewing it as preparation for the new door God's going to open for you. The tension of these strong refining moments becomes too much to bear because you don't understand why it's happening to you.

If, during a moment of discomfort, a door opens that's not from God, you'll probably walk straight through it without talking to Him about it in an attempt to get out of this season. I've seen people walk through damaging doors just to escape their current situation instead of asking God to uncover the reason for their season. It only led them to a dead end and questioning God.

If you're asking God for understanding, the next steps are to listen for God's voice, be obedient, and watch how He responds, even if it doesn't meet your expectations. You won't be let down if you don't have expectations. God knows what's best for you, so have faith that everything will work out for His glory. Wait and watch how He moves in your life next. If it's for you, you won't have to force it. He'll do all the work!

Discernment

The last thing you should include in your prayers is seeking discernment. To discern something means having the ability to recognize small details, accurately telling the difference between similar things, and making wise judgments by using such observations. As a believer, we have to be able to judge between right and wrong, discern the truth and the lies, and identify what's good and what's bad. This doesn't just apply to bigger issues that go against God's Word, but even in the smaller, less complex issues.

You can have supernatural knowledge and understanding, but if you're not able to discern His will in every situation, things can still lead you astray. There is a real war taking place in the spiritual realm. One of the greatest tactics used by the enemy is the art of distraction. In the middle of what God is doing, the enemy will try to pull your focus off God so that you don't live out your purpose. When you follow your purpose with commitment, it interferes with the enemy's plans. Of course, he wants you to be distracted.

The enemy will come after your finances, attack your family, showcase gratifying opportunities to disrupt your life, and present anything shiny to grab your attention. Asking God to help you recognize and discern what's from Him and what's not from Him will determine your next season. When you ask for discernment, you're asking God to give you the ability to accurately tell the difference between the doors He's opening and closing. It means you're asking God to help you identify what's true and what's false. Praying that God sharpens your discernment helps equip you with the right tools to take the right actions to move in the right direction. You may have knowledge of God's will and you may have biblical understanding of what's going on in your life, but when you're faced with warning signs, you may still cross over the caution tape because you lack discernment.

More Than a Wish List

Praying for knowledge, understanding, and discernment is a significant part of my prayer life. That kind of prayer goes past superficial conversation, and it has helped strengthen and deepen my relationship with God. God wants me to use my knowledge, He wants me to process and understand His ways, and He wants me to use discernment in all my actions, thoughts, and behaviors. Applying these tools produces spiritual growth and maturity.

As a kid, each year for Christmas I would make a wish list of the things I wanted. My list included typical gifts that most kids desire: a bicycle, video games, an entertainment system, toys that flew, action figures, army trucks, a football, and remote-control cars. I would even go as far as cutting out pictures from newspaper ads and gluing them onto a big poster, like a giant Christmas gift board. Though I didn't need any of these things, I wanted them. I felt they would add value to my life. The wish lists I made came from a place of immaturity and a lack of life experience. I wanted things that would be exciting and fun.

When Christmas Day came around, I'd open my presents only to find a few things on my list. Profound disappointment usually crept in, and it robbed my joy and appreciation for the items I did receive. At the time, I didn't understand that my mom couldn't afford the other expensive toys. My attention was on what I was lacking and the comparison of the number of gifts I got versus the other kids in my grade. As I grew older and became more mature, it was easier to understand why I didn't get everything on my Christmas wish list.

The same goes for our spiritual growth and maturity. We may not understand why God doesn't give us everything we ask Him for, but in time it all will make perfect sense. As I look back at my life, I'm so thankful things have gone God's way and not mine. Though many things were contrary to my wants, God always provided me with everything I needed. When I look back at those Christmases, I can remember receiving gifts from my grandma that were things that I needed, not what I wanted.

Every Christmas Day, there would be a long, flat box from JCPenney that had no wrapping paper. I knew what was inside before even opening it, because it was the same JCPenney box my grandma always sent gifts in. It was always the first present my mom made me open because she knew I wouldn't be excited about what was inside.

Inside would be a pair of pajamas, a couple packages of socks, and a couple packages of underwear. After quickly opening it, I would give my grandma a hug, toss the items aside, and open the other presents I deemed more important. Though I didn't realize it at the time, I used those essential items every day after Christmas. In her wisdom, my grandmother knew the value of her gift.

As God gives us the things that we need, we start to see the value in asking for things that line up with His will. We have to remember that if we don't have it, we don't need it. Being content with what we have exhibits spiritual growth.

My prayers are no longer filled with lists of desires. My prayers come from a position of acknowledging my needs. As I do so, I often realize that many of the answers to my prayers are right in front of me. When I stopped being so consumed with trying to pray my way out of certain situations or praying for things to go my way, I started asking for the right things. I've accepted the fact that the place I'm in is preparing me for what's next. The situations I'm facing are refining me and providing everything I need to complete the mission God has for me. If we truly trust God and have faith that He is in control, then our prayer life should reflect that heart posture.

What do your prayers sound like? What are you asking for? When you adjust the way you pray, you start to see that

God hears you, that He is answering, that He is providing, and that He always knows what's best. Before my spiritual growth, I used to have a victim mentality. I believed that God didn't hear my prayers or that He had abandoned me. Now I know God has me right where He *needs* me. It's my privilege to be used as His vessel to help fulfill God's Kingdom work.

PRAYER FOR KNOWLEDGE, UNDERSTANDING AND DISCERNMENT

Father God, I know that You hear my prayer. Today I ask that You give me knowledge, understanding, and discernment. Help me to have the knowledge to see that the change I'm asking You for has already been given to me—I just need to see it through Your lens. Please grant me the ability to understand this season, to understand the environment I've been placed in, to understand my feelings, and to better understand my actions and reactions. Help me to understand that I'm fully equipped and have everything I need for today to be victorious, because I'm a vessel for the Holy Spirit. Help me to utilize discernment, seeing through the tactics of the enemy and shifting my mindset in a way that helps me view every obstacle as an opportunity. Lord, help me to make righteous decisions that are in alignment with Your will, even if it's uncomfortable and uneasy. Father, continue to guide me. Please open doors that are only from You, and close all doors that are not from You. I only desire to walk through doors that You open. I pray this in Jesus' mighty name, Amen.

APPLICATION

1. How does this chapter challenge your current prayer life? Do you find yourself praying for a list of things you want God to do, or are you asking for Him to change you?

2. Identify what God is trying to reveal to you in this current season. What areas of your life can you identify that He's trying to change: your perspective, a characteristic trait, your heart posture?

3. As you pray this week, be intentional about having God shift your perspective from changing your circumstances to changing you.

THIRTEEN

How to Know When God Is Answering Your Prayers Indirectly

God has a way of turning our mess into a miracle. We cannot limit the way God moves or how He answers prayers. His ways are higher than our ways because He's the Author of our lives. We can't see the big picture because we're only a small piece of a large puzzle, a grain of sand on a beach, a drop of water in the entire ocean. There's no way we can identify what God is doing in the tiny details of our lives. Many times, God is answering our prayers in ways we can't think of or imagine. He's always working behind the scenes weaving things together for our good and His glory (see Romans 8:28).

Have you ever looked back at your life only to realize how God pieced your circumstances together for good? Maybe you can identify how He orchestrated certain jobs and opportunities in your favor. Maybe you can highlight moments when He made sure you crossed paths with other people who added value to your life. Maybe He removed obstacles and replaced them with better options. Maybe He intertwined occasions that led to further connection and fellowship that you needed.

Can you see how He has opened and closed doors, how He's protected and redirected you, and how He has healed broken pieces? He always has and always will work in your life, even when you don't see it. You have to remember that God doesn't operate according to our schedules, our goals, or our expectations. He only operates on His perfect timing in His perfect way.

God Is Never Late

When I was 23, my church had a weeklong revival. Each night a different evangelist taught and shared a prophetic word with whomever God called them to speak to. I made sure I attended each night in the hopes that a prophetic word would be spoken over my life. As the revival services went on, people were getting called to the front of the congregation by different evangelists. It was almost as if they had won the lottery. I said a prayer every night before walking into the revival service asking God to open opportunities for my future so that I could experience financial breakthroughs. I put all my eggs into this basket, hoping an evangelist would call me up and a miracle would happen in my life. As the seventh night ended, no prophetic words had been spoken over me. I started to feel discouraged, thinking God didn't want to answer my prayer.

Just before the pastor approached the stage to end the service, the evangelist looked at me and asked me to come up front. As I walked to the front, I thought to myself, *This is it, my prayer is going to get answered. This is when my life changes.* The preacher laid his hands on my shoulder and said, "Young man, you're called to ministry. You have words of gold, and you will speak to millions of people about Jesus."

My heart nearly stopped. I was not expecting those words to come out of his mouth. All I could do was nod my head and walk away. I was sure he had the wrong guy. My heart was not set on ministry or preaching the Word of God. I only wanted to attend church—not serve in ministry my whole life. I had my own dreams, goals, and visions for my life. Plus, I didn't even know a million people. The only friends I had were those in my community and thirteen friends on MySpace. Not to mention that I despised public speaking. I had no idea where "words of gold" would come from.

Fast-forward twelve years. I've watched God fulfill the exact prophecy He gave me. I went on to follow my calling in ministry in the exact order the prophetic word was spoken over me. A prayer that I prayed asking God to open opportunities for my future was answered. It just wasn't answered how I was expecting it to be answered. God isn't trapped by time or our expectations, so even though it took twelve years for an answer to my prayer to come to pass, it was in alignment with His schedule, His perfect timing, and His will. I needed to experience a ton of failures, overcome obstacles, and make it through self-inflicted life lessons first. God knew exactly what He was doing letting twelve years go by before allowing me to step into my calling. He first needed to prune me, prepare me, refine me, and whittle away the rough edges of my character before this prayer could be answered.

Now, after having been in ministry for few years, becoming a pastor, a church planter, an author, and using the speaking gift God has given me to tell millions of people about Jesus, I can say with confidence that God answers prayers indirectly. An indirect prayer is a prayer answered, but not according to your expectations or timeline.

I wish I had received this spiritual guidance when I was twenty-three and was new in my faith. To know that God answers every prayer means He's always listening and hasn't left you. He will give you what your heart desires if it's in alignment with His will. He will reject some prayers for your protection. He will redirect some prayers so that you can fall into your calling. He will answer your prayers indirectly. If you're a new believer, stay tuned into the frequency of God and how He's moving in your life. Don't ignore messages He's trying to send you because you're too focused on yourself.

The Path of Resistance and Distractions

When God was leading the children of Israel through the wilderness (see Exodus 13), it was easy to see where He was taking them because a cloud gathered in the daytime and a pillar of fire appeared at night. This cloud and pillar moved when it was time to pack up and relocate (see Exodus 13:21–22). Whenever the cloud or fire moved, the Israelites would follow. When it was time to stay, the cloud and fire stayed put. These signs provided a visible, tangible reminder of the presence of God. There was no mistaking what God wanted them to do—all they needed was to watch the cloud or pillar of fire.

While we don't have tangible signs such as these, God does show us when and how to follow Him. I believe He makes it evident when He answers our prayers or leads us in a new direction. Sometimes you can anticipate the movement of God by noticing when things seem to be getting more diffi-cult or off course in your life. When you're playing a video game, for example, the closer you get to completing a level, the more opposition you will experience. As things try to stop you from getting to the finish line, you can receive it as confirmation that you're heading in the right direction. If you're playing the video game and you accidentally turn yourself around and backtrack, you will not experience op-position because you're not close to the finish line. There's no need to stop you.

What I've experienced in my own walk with God is that there is more spiritual warfare, resistance, and opposition the closer I get to where God wants me to go. If I'm off track and out of alignment with God, why would the enemy resist me? He has me right where he wants me. I'm not following my purpose. I'm not walking in the fullness of my author-ity. If I'm lost, wandering off track and not keeping my eyes locked on Jesus, that's essentially a victory for the enemy. The enemy wants us to remain stuck. He doesn't want us to fulfill our calling.

When I dedicate myself to reading my Bible every day, spending extra alone time to sit in God's presence, pruning and auditing the activities in my life that are causing a hin-drance, and keeping my eyes focused on Jesus, that is when I have experienced the most resistance. I start to accept that when God is about to move or redirect me through a new season, I'm probably going to experience some warfare. That's when I know I'm heading in the right direction.

When this happens to you, stay on course. Do not get discouraged! Use this time to draw even closer to God in obedience and the pursuit of righteousness. Don't give in to the temptation to quit, and do not get sidetracked. Remember: "Trust in the LORD with all your heart and lean not on your own understanding; in all your ways submit to him, and he will make your paths straight" (Proverbs 3:5–6).

Another way we can recognize that God is moving is when we notice an abundance of opportunity. I've noticed in my life that as God is trying to guide me through one specific door, several other doors of opportunity randomly open. It reminds me of one of those crazy mazes at a carnival where you must choose between three doors, and only one of them leads you out of the maze. The other two are meant to cause distraction, delay, or confusion.

I've been in situations when God was leading me in one direction, and as I was preparing to go that way, new and more lucrative opportunities arose out of nowhere—even though God was calling me in a different direction. The allure and promise of bigger and better either delayed my response, confused me, or completely captured my attention.

I remember that just a few weeks after I received a prophetic word that I was called to ministry, I was offered a full-ride scholarship to play basketball at a local community college. A friend of mine invited me to come play at an exhibition game against the college's basketball team. The coach of that team was watching the players and the competition. After a few games, the coach approached me.

Within minutes, he offered me a full-ride scholarship to play on his team.

This opportunity pulled at my heartstrings, because one of my deepest desires and dreams had been to play basketball at college level. So, instead of pursuing the calling on my life in ministry, I took what I thought at the time was a once-in-a-lifetime opportunity to do something I had dreamed of doing. In that moment, it wasn't a hard decision. I packed everything up and left the church. In other words, I packed everything up and left God.

This illustrates God's love, mercy, grace, and sovereignty, because even though I didn't choose Him or my calling at that time, He still worked all things together for good. "And we know that in all things God works for the good of those who love him, who have been called according to his purpose" (Romans 8:28).

I believe that had I stayed on track, God would have used me in mighty ways. But because I have free will, I chose a different path. The beauty is that my decision didn't change His love for me. He used the time I spent going in the opposite direction to build my testimony.

When ministering to people, I always encourage them to be alert and aware of sudden opportunities, especially when they are getting closer to the Lord. Not every opportunity is from God. The enemy will put shiny new toys in front of you, hoping you'll take the bait and get confused. Don't get distracted by these things. God is about to move in your life to develop you as a vessel for the Holy Spirit as child of God.

God is not a God of confusion. Where He wants you to go and what He wants you to do will always come with confirmation. That's why it's important for us to seek godly counsel, stay rooted in Scripture, spend time in prayer, and take time to quiet ourselves so that we can truly hear the voice of God. Remember, God is not going to yell at you to get your attention. He's a Gentleman.

Every time God has answered a prayer of mine or led me in a specific direction, I have always received confirmation. As you're praying for wisdom, understanding, and discernment, you'll be able to recognize God's confirmations. When you allow the outcome to be His outcome and not your outcome, you have received His confirmation. If you have to lie or manipulate to make things go a certain way, that's not from God. When it comes to His will, God wants us to have faith in how He moves. When He lays out the final confirmation to the direction He's given us, we don't want to ignore it or make poor decisions.

We are reactive creatures who tend to jump at every opportunity, break down at the first sign of resistance, and rush forward through every door that opens. I believe that when we ask, especially when it comes to His guidance, He will always reveal His truth. When we ignore Him, which we've all been guilty of doing, we end up in our own self-perpetuated construction zone.

Many times, God gives us clear confirmation to follow in His purpose, whether that's through godly counsel, reading Scripture, or removing opportunities. When His direction is not what we want, we ignore His voice and bulldoze our way in the direction we want to go. We begin to rationalize our behavior, question the plan God has for us, and manipulate Scripture so that our choices and decisions fit our personal agenda. Then we wonder why we keep making the same mistakes. We wonder why we lack purpose, peace, comfort, joy, and fullness.

The answer is because we're in a place to which God never called us. We're in a place into which we squeezed and forced ourselves. We ignored God because we believed we knew better than He did. God is moving and answering your prayers. It's important that you listen and pay attention to His confirmation. Obey what He's saying, even if it's not what you expected. It is better to spend one day pursuing His purpose for your life than a thousand days somewhere else.

God Knows Best

You need to write "God knows best" on the tablet of your heart every day. He's the One who designed you. How can you forget that? God is a God of provision. He always provides what you need to fulfill His purpose. Let that sink in for just a moment. If you don't have something, you must not need it to be who He's called you to be.

This is a challenging concept. Many of us look at this world and only see what we're lacking. We might feel that if we get the things our heart desires, we will be complete. That is putting our hope, faith, and trust in material things. Ultimately, the things of this world are counterfeit and will never satisfy or fulfill you.

If you only had the next twenty-four hours to live, how would you spend your time? Would you be concerned with objects and material things, or would you spend your last day with God? Every day that you have air in your lungs is a blessing, and your purpose is to use that breath to make Him more known and to bring Him glory.

God doesn't want us to stress, overthink, worry, or accumulate items. When we become obsessed with worldly success, fill our schedules with things that are non-essential, and become self-focused and goal-oriented, we overlook what God wants to do. God makes sure that we're fully equipped each day to fulfill the plan He's laid out before us. We can't focus on yesterday. If we're focusing on our past, guilt, shame, or regrets, we will be rendered useless.

There's nothing wrong with reflecting on yesterday and sharing our testimony to bring glory to God, but we have to remember that we've been made new, and He wants to do something in this moment. There's nothing wrong with setting goals, having a vision, or planning for the future. Goals help pave a way in your life. The problem arises when we become so consumed with our yesterdays and tomorrows that we miss the gift of today and what God is trying to do in it. This is why it's very important to pay attention to areas of spiritual warfare, resistance, and opposition.

Many times, the areas of your life where you're experiencing these things are the areas you need to double down on spending time with God, reading Scripture, completing your devotionals, and seeking godly wisdom from a brother or sister in Christ. Finding an accountability partner who can pray for you and help in your spiritual walk will also be beneficial in times of opposition. Don't get distracted by every shiny new opportunity that presents itself. Make sure you receive confirmation through prayer, godly counsel, and the Word of God to make sure those opportunities aren't distractions.

You were made for this specific moment, and if you don't have everything you want, God must have a different objective for you. Stay focused and in alignment with Him and know that He's always answering your prayers. He may answer them immediately, later, or indirectly. Your heart should want God's answered prayers on His timing and in His way, because He always knows best.

PRAYER FOR HIS WILL TO BE DONE

Heavenly Father, I ask that Your will would be done in my life. Help me to set aside my limitations, my finite resources, and my small expectations. Move as You see fit, and help me to see things as You do. Forgive me for placing You in a box and trying to see You through the lens of humanity. You are God! You are mighty! You take what is impossible and make it possible. So, have Your way in my situation. Move the mountains and part the seas. I surrender my expectations and pray that You would breathe life into my prayers according to Your purpose. I pray this with the authority given to me by my Lord and Savior. In Jesus' name, Amen.

APPLICATION

1. When has God answered your prayers indirectly or in a way that wasn't how you expected? What did you learn about God and His method of answering prayers?
2. How easily are you distracted or led astray? How can you better safeguard yourself from being taken down the wrong road?

3. This week while you're praying, be more open to God's answers. Be mindful that He's not limited by your resources and abilities. After you pray, surrender and let go of the expectations and narrow views you might be placing around God's response.

FOURTEEN

The Blessing of the Closed Door

When I was eleven years old, I met my dad for the very first time. I was shocked at how tall he was. He was six feet six. I had heard stories about how he had played basketball in high school and college. I collected newspaper articles highlighting him scoring thirty, forty, and even fifty points in games. He was a baller.

With basketball being my dad's comfort sport, the first thing he did when I met him was take me to the park to shoot some hoops. He wanted to use that time for us to get to know each other better. Unfortunately, I had never played basketball. It had never crossed my mind because I didn't have the guidance or instruction on how to get involved in children's sports and activities. Not to mention, I was about five feet eleven and close to two hundred and twenty pounds. My body was built like an offensive lineman. I had zero coordination and couldn't dribble a basketball.

As my dad and I started playing, I kept bouncing the ball off my feet. I couldn't make a basic layup, and I kept looking down at the ball when I was dribbling instead of looking forward. Once he realized that I had never touched a basketball, my dad became increasingly frustrated and short with me. After several moments of me fumbling around on the court, he said something to me I never forgot. He said, "I thought you were my son." This forever changed the trajectory of my life.

Although this was the first and last interaction I had with my dad, this painful experience ignited the fire and passion within me to develop my skills as a basketball player. As we left the court that day, I felt discouraged, sad, and rejected, but that moment was the driving force behind me becoming obsessed with the game. I was now motivated to prove my dad wrong and prove that I was his son.

The introduction to this sport turned out to be an integral part of my growth and development as a man. Unfortunately, as I grew to excel in basketball, going on to play in high school and college, my dad never came to see me play. But when one door closes, another door opens, all for the glory of His name.

One Door Closes, Another Door Opens

Looking back, I can see all the doors God opened in my life and how many doors He had to shut for my protection or redirection. Though the door to my relationship with my dad closed, God opened more doors and more opportunities. For instance, the door to advancing my skill in basketball opened that granted me the opportunity to receive a full-ride scholarship to play basketball at a four-year university. From there, I went on to earn a bachelor's degree, which opened the opportunity for me to become a business owner. God was always working and weaving the intricate details of my life together.

One summer, while playing basketball in college, I was introduced to a sport called CrossFit. Our head coach brought in his wife, who was a strength and conditioning coach, and she introduced us to this new form of discipline training. I immediately fell in love with CrossFit. I began an internship with my coach's wife and gained even more appreciation for the sport. After I received my degree, I partnered with her to open my own CrossFit gym. Though I didn't continue to pursue my career in basketball, which felt like leaving a piece of me behind, I did go on to become a business owner. This became a new passion of mine.

God used my season in college basketball to strengthen me, develop me, and realign me with my purpose in ministry. Closing the door to basketball and opening the door to becoming a gym owner was God's way of redirecting me to the path He wanted me on. God's plans are always greater than ours. The beauty of reflection and looking back at your life is that you're able to see exactly how God moved, why He was shifting, why He was replacing, why He was removing, and how He was protecting you, redirecting you, refining you, preparing you, and keeping you from settling for less than what you deserve. God is always orchestrating this spiritual symphony in our lives, and He always brings things full circle. Trust that when one door closes, another door will open according to His will.

Asking God to Close Doors

When God closes a door, it may seem as if He's not working or that you're getting the short end of the stick. It can make you feel as if your heart is being torn out of your chest. It can be discouraging and make no sense. But we have to remember that when He closes a door, it's closed. He's closed it for a reason.

God does all things on His schedule according to His will. Anything we do on our own time and outside His will falls on us. We can't say that He's not listening to us or that He doesn't love us. We can't play the victim and start questioning Him when things don't work out the way we expected. If we act on our own, we can only blame ourselves for failed relationships, failed career choices, failed home relocations, and failed business deals. That's why when God says no, His answer has love written all over it.

Our heavenly Father loves us and always wants what's best for us; therefore, to avoid heartache, disaster, and feeling as though life is unfair, ask God to close doors that aren't from Him. That way when He closes a door, it will be easier to accept.

One of my regular prayers is, *Lord, close any doors that You don't want me to walk through. Help me to discern which open doors are from You and which are not. Give me the understanding and knowledge to handle closed doors so that I can continue to be a good steward for Your work.* When you accept closed doors, it becomes easier to trust His guidance, and it starts to fill you with love, knowing you have a 24/7 Protector. He sees things that you can't, He knows what's being said when you're not around, He knows who is planning on hurting you, He knows who is lying to you, and He knows what will break you.

His no is for the greater good of your life, and it's always for His glory. When your heart is in the right place, you no longer want to make choices and decisions that don't align with where He wants you to go. I've spent too much time going in the opposite direction, and I know where that ends up. I'm thankful that God will take the mess we make and turn it into a miracle.

How much further could we go if we were obedient? How much more could we achieve if we received His no the same way we received His *yes*? I believe we waste a lot of time mourning the answers to our prayers. We say that we trust God and have faith, and yet we waste precious moments grumbling and complaining about the things that we didn't get. "Hope deferred makes the heart sick, but a longing fulfilled is a tree of life" (Proverbs 13:12).

God doesn't tell us no so that He can watch us suffer, or struggle, or because He doesn't love us. It's time to come back to that place of complete submission and surrender, trusting that when God says no, there is purpose behind it. There will be attacks from the enemy, and you will experience spiritual warfare. There will be things sent your way that will try to take you out, steal your focus, and knock you off track.

Despite the enemy's greatest efforts, if you keep your eyes on Jesus and stay aware, you can overcome anything. "No weapon formed against you shall prosper" (Isaiah 54:17 NKJV). This means weapons will form, but they will not prevail. Weapons used against you can be disguised as things that you want. This is another reason God doesn't give us everything we want. He's trying to protect us from things that can cause major damage and disruption in our lives.

Many of us don't even know what we need. We think we know what will help us, what will heal us, and what will change us, but only God knows. In the scope of eternity, we're little children, and our Father knows best. I'm constantly reminding myself that if I'm not getting what I'm asking for, it's because God is protecting me from something I can't see: the relationships He didn't allow me to get into, the friendships He let dissolve, the move He never let me make, the career He didn't let me advance in, or the job opportunity He didn't offer me. These could have all been weapons forming that He didn't let prosper. Whatever does or does not happen, God has His reasons.

Not all weapons that form are hidden; some are visible. Have you ever had someone betray you? Have you ever had someone attack your character? Have you ever had someone threaten you? If yes, then you've personally seen weapons form right before your eyes. How you respond to weapons is important. "You have heard that it was said, 'Eye for eye, and tooth for tooth.' But I tell you, do not resist an evil person. If anyone slaps you on the right cheek, turn to them the other cheek also" (Matthew 5:38–39). We're told to turn the other cheek when we feel attacked or when the circumstance feels unfair and unjust. Even though we want to get rid of the weapons ourselves, we must trust in the power of our heavenly Father. He will not allow any of those weapons to succeed. There's no need to stress, worry, or be anxious.

God Doesn't Make Mistakes

We are creatures who crave instant gratification because we are incredibly shortsighted. The world we live in caters to that desire. With just the click of a button, we can have about anything delivered to our doorsteps in less than an hour. Conditioned to having easy access to everything, we try to apply this tendency to our relationship with God. We lack patience, get antsy, rush into decisions, and throw temper tantrums when something we want doesn't happen. But we must remember that God doesn't make mistakes.

A good friend of mine who is a pastor shared a story with me. He said that early in his ministry, he had a very lucrative job opportunity to take over a thriving and growing church. If he chose to accept the position, he would have had to pack his whole house and move his family across the country. It came with a salary that was three times what he was currently making, a fully furnished home, and great health benefits. It was an amazing setup that would have changed his family's life.

Rather than rushing into the opportunity, he prayed over it. He kept hearing the Holy Spirit say no. He couldn't quite wrap his mind around it, but as he continued to pray, he continued to hear a very strong no. He even laid down a fleece for confirmation (see Judges 6). Though there weren't any red flags that popped up, he declined the offer out of obedience to the Spirit. He received a lot of criticism, and many people questioned his decision. They felt it was foolish of him to pass up such an opportunity. But he knew he had done the right thing because he was at peace.

After he decided to stay in his current role, the Lord instructed him to continue building and growing his current ministry. Less than a year later, he got word that the thriving church where he had been offered the position had closed its doors due to scandals related to immorality, improper use of funds, and other moral failures. Had he taken that job based on the outer appearance and what he thought he wanted, he and his family would have been caught in the middle of those scandals. God didn't allow him to rush into something that looked good on the outside but was rotten at the core. His obedience to God's direction protected him and his family. This testimony is a great reminder that *no* is an answer to our prayers. God makes no mistakes; only we do.

The reason I believe God reveals His plans to us in small increments is because if we saw the overall big picture of our lives, many of us would try to avoid all the difficult moments. Life is challenging, uncomfortable, filled with treacherous terrain, and is littered with obstacles, suffering, pain, hard times, and tragedy. If we knew how everything was going to play out, both the good and the ugly, we would be scared, sad, and probably rendered paralyzed by the hard moments ahead. I believe God takes us down these paths using gentle nudges. We experience different kinds of emotions, so our focus keeps returning to Him and the greater good He has for our lives. If we knew how our lives were going to play out, we would have no reason to depend on Him in all that we do.

We need to rely on Him to open doors, to shut down opportunities that aren't from Him, to remove people from our lives, and to replace things that we need. The things we go through help us mature, adjust our heart posture, and reevaluate our desires. Let's say an opportunity doesn't pan out your way. Your reaction will highlight your motives. Do you want everything to go your way, or do you accept when things go His way? God often redirects us by canceling or preventing something from happening. God's character is love.

"I am the light of the world. He who follows Me shall not walk in darkness, but have the light of life" (John 8:12 NKJV).

God shines His light on the paths we walk down so that we aren't walking in darkness. The world is a dark place because so many people aren't following God's light. The world is hurting because people don't know Jesus. There's a Jesus-shaped hole in every human's heart that only He can fill. Knowing this, I want to go through each season holding His hand and having the understanding, wisdom, and discernment that will help me overcome each battle.

I saw a powerful illustration on social media recently. There was an image of a little girl hugging her stuffed teddy bear tightly while Jesus was right in front of her kneeling down with one hand out signaling for her to give Him the bear. She didn't want to hand Jesus the bear because it was her favorite bear, and she didn't want to be left with nothing. What she didn't know was that behind Jesus' back, in His other hand, He had a much larger bear that He wanted to give her in exchange.

This paints a beautiful picture of our relationship with Jesus. We often hold on to things that are smaller or less than what God wants us to have. In our fear and insecurity, we don't want to surrender or submit the important things in our lives because we're scared that we might not get them back, or we're unsure of how we'll be able to move on. This stuffed teddy bear represents relationships, material things, parts of our identity and self-worth, habits, addictions, routines, schedules, and so much more.

Many of us settle for less than what we deserve without realizing it. This is often because we've been let down, chewed up, and spit out by the world. Our self-worth, value, and identity are mixed up in the things we do, what we own, and traumatic events we experience. We're scared to let go and let God. We think that we'll lose ourselves or maybe forget who we are. The truth is that God wants to give us a new identity, help us find our value and worth in Him, and exchange those dead things for greater things.

When God closes a door, He's protecting us from unknown hurts. He's redirecting us to be in alignment with His plan, and He's keeping us from settling. In the book of Luke, we read the story of the prodigal son (see Luke 15). A son asks his father for his inheritance. Once he receives it, he blows all the money on a frivolous lifestyle. With no fortune left and nothing to show for it, the son finds himself having to find work feeding pigs. He couldn't afford food, so when he got hungry, he would eat the slop that the pigs ate.

After being settled there for a while, the son remembered who he was and where he came from. He swallowed his pride and returned to his father's house. He realized he had done wrong, so he changed his mindset and heart posture. When he returned home, his father saw him, ran out to embrace him, placed a ring on his finger, put new shoes on his feet, and clothed him in a robe. He killed the fattest calf and threw a celebration for the return of his son.

The prodigal son had been settling for far less than what God had created him for. Even after his mistakes, even after his blunders, even after his carelessness, he remained an heir. In the same way, we must remember that even though our past might be filled with regrets, guilt, shameful acts, and a host of mistakes and failures, because of what Jesus did on the cross, we are children of God who have been forgiven. "'For I know the plans I have for you,' declares the LORD, 'plans to prosper you and not to harm you, plans to give you hope and a future'" (Jeremiah 29:11).

God created you for a relationship with Him. That relationship was not just for eternity, but for this life on earth. He has plans to prosper you. He wants more for you than you want for yourself. Embrace both open and closed doors, knowing His plans for you are good and so much better than what you could accomplish on your own.

PRAYER FOR CLOSED DOORS

Heavenly Father, give me eyes to see that Your hands are orchestrating my life. Help me to step back and remember that You are in total control. Lord, I trust You with my life. I surrender and submit full control to You. I'm asking for closed doors today. Close any doors that weren't opened by You. Shut down opportunities that are meant to lead me astray. If anything is coming my way that's not from You, I don't want it. Help me to handle discouragement, sadness, and disappointment in a way that doesn't distract or sideline me. I need You. Thank You for protecting me, redirecting me, and keeping me from settling for less than what You have created me for. In Jesus' name, Amen.

APPLICATION

1. When have you experienced being really excited about something and the door was closed on it? How

did it make you feel in the moment? What was your reaction? How did it affect your prayer life?

2. On the other hand, how did you see the way God protected you or redirected you through that closed door? How did you feel? Did it build your trust? How did it affect your faith in God?

3. Knowing that God is in control and wants what's best for you, how can you better handle disappointment or bad news? In what ways can you see the good in the bad?

4. What closed doors are you struggling with right now and having a hard time seeing the good? How can you apply this chapter to change your perspective on closed doors?

FIFTEEN

What to Do When Your Prayers Are Answered

Every prayer I've ever prayed in my life has been answered by God. I can say with confidence that God has never left me hanging, and He has provided an answer to my every prayer. I can't say that I've always been happy with His answers or that I've always received everything I asked for, but I've learned to trust God's answers. I've learned that *no* and *not right now* are answers, too.

I've experienced an immediate *yes* to my prayers, I've seen God close doors to something I was praying for, I've had God step in and show me how to change the way I was asking for things, and I've also had to wait years for a prayer to be answered. I've been through it all, and because of that, I now understand that no matter what, it's my spiritual duty to pray and seek His answers. "For everyone who asks receives; the one who seeks finds; and to the one who knocks, the door will be opened" (Matthew 7:8). When we knock on God's door, He will open it. When we seek His answers, He will provide them in His way.

I'll never forget the moment I encountered the Holy Spirit and knew God was real. I was in the eighth grade and had heard a lot of talk about a higher power. I wasn't sure where I stood on the topic since I hadn't grown up in church. One day I was at a basketball court behind the school that was adjacent to my house. I was throwing shots but kept missing. I was getting frustrated because I was spending more time running around chasing the ball all over the schoolyard than I was making shots. Internally, I started talking to myself negatively, using thoughts to beat myself up, and creating dialogues that eroded my self-worth.

To help build my confidence, I started playing a mental game with myself. As I prepared to shoot the next ball, I said to myself, "If I make this shot, then I'll play in the NBA." I shot and the ball completely missed the rim. I retrieved it and started squeezing the ball, making angry huffing and puffing noises, and then threw the ball at the side of a nearby barn.

After I chased the ball down again, I went back to the court and tried again. With each new shot, I inched my way closer to the rim and made a new wish. Finally, I said, "If I make this shot, then I'm going to be rich." The ball hit the rim, circled it, and bounced out. Of course, the ball didn't go in. I was beyond mad at this point.

With dozens of missed shots, I was filled with spite, frustration, and disappointment. I decided to try one more shot, this time making my mental challenge intentionally evil. I grabbed the ball, moved as far away from the rim as I could, looked at the rim and said, "If I don't make this, there is no

God." I said this with all certainty that the ball wouldn't go in. As I launched the basketball from the free-throw line on the other side of the court, I watched the ball move in slow motion straight into the hoop without touching the rim. I was astonished.

My stomach dropped, I got choked up, and chills went up and down my arms. An eerie feeling came over me as I looked around. I saw no one. I remember grabbing my basketball and running home with a sense of panic. This was one of the first supernatural experiences I can recall when I had a moment between me and God. I went seeking for an answer from a higher power, and even though I was a young, lost kid who didn't have a relationship with God, He still provided a *response* in His way that allowed me to feel the Holy Spirit within me.

I can write a long, sad story about all the ways God didn't answer my prayers the way I wanted Him to, but that would put the spotlight on me and take away from God's glory. God should receive all the glory for everything He does in our lives. I'm thankful things haven't always gone my way or that I haven't gotten everything I've wanted. If everything had gone my way, I wouldn't be where I am today. The old me used to take control of every decision, ignore every sign from God, and act disobediently. I always ran myself into a ditch. I didn't make the right decisions and choices, I didn't see things through a spiritual lens, and I let my emotions and feelings get the best of me.

Now I can see my walk with God. I can identify His sovereignty, power, and protection over my life. I'm able to discern and recognize that He answers my prayers by placing confirmations in my spirit. The Holy Spirit serves as a Counselor, a Guide, and a Helper. I know that when God answers my prayer, the Holy Spirit leads me to that conclusion.

If the answer is a *yes*, I usually see the tangible evidence. If the answer is a *no*, I feel a sense of acceptance and protection. If the answer is *not yet*, I feel content in my spirit knowing that the door isn't fully closed and there's just a barrier in front of it for now. It's my responsibility to come to grips with whatever the answer is and continue to press into God for the next instruction.

An Attitude of Gratitude

In the Bible, we are called to be grateful in all circumstances. "Give thanks in all circumstances; for this is God's will for you in Christ Jesus" (1 Thessalonians 5:18). This means having gratitude despite ups and downs, highs and lows, during seasons of abundance and provision, and in seasons of storms and disturbance. Having the same gratitude in seasons of turmoil as we do in seasons of growth showcases our faith.

It can be hard to be grateful when you feel you're lacking so much. You can struggle tremendously if you don't keep your eyes on our heavenly Father. You can feel easily burdened because you can't find gratitude for the things you do have. In those circumstances, prioritizing God feels more like a chore than an absolute privilege. Every day you must readjust and reevaluate your heart posture. Every day you must count your blessings. Every day you must remind yourself you've already received the greatest gift: salvation.

If God never answered another one of your prayer requests, He's already done enough for you. For that, you are blessed and highly favored. Disappointment and discouragement can creep in on us easily when we look at everyone else's lives. That's why practicing gratitude daily brings us to a place of humility and helps us realign ourselves with the truth of who God is and who He says we are.

It's easy to be grateful when we have victories, achievements, and accomplishments to celebrate. During the seasons of abundance and provision, we find it effortless to thank God for those high, pivotal moments. These moments should be celebrated, and we should show our gratitude to the Lord for carrying us through to those achievements.

When we make those achievements about ourselves, we no longer bring glory to Him. Yes, you may have put in the work, but God deserves all the glory for those great wins in your life. He should be celebrated! He should be exalted! Without Him, those victories wouldn't have been possible.

When God answers a prayer, tell someone about it. Share with someone the goodness of God and all that He has done in your life. The more we celebrate Him for everything in our lives, the more we bring honor and glory to His name. In doing so, more people will see His grace and love, and more people will hear about the amazing God we have the privilege of serving.

All Glory to God

One of my favorite Bible verses is found in Revelation 12:11. It says, "They triumphed over him by the blood of the Lamb and by the word of their testimony; they did not love their lives so much as to shrink from death." One of our absolute privileges as followers of Jesus is to share our testimony. When we tell others about the things God has carried us through and helped us overcome, His name is glorified. Our testimony is our personal witness of who God is and what He has done in our lives.

It's irrefutable. No one can tell me what my experience has or has not been. People can refute scientific evidence and they can come up with arguments to try to disprove the existence of God, but they cannot refute my personal life experience and testimony.

When God answers my prayers, I'm gifted with the opportunity to testify to it. When my prayers are answered according to God's will, there's always purpose in it. When I share my life story, it's filled with closed doors, open doors, deferred dreams, unimaginable opportunities, consequences, and victories. All the outcomes showcase the goodness and love of God. Everything that I've gone through and experienced adds to my testimony and creates more opportunity for me to reach people with the Gospel.

Have you heard the saying that life is a journey? It's so true. This life we're given is a journey, and it's not over until we breathe our last breath. There will be countless things that God carries you through, holds your hand through, and walks with you through. Once you make it over the mountain, there will be another mountain to climb. If God doesn't completely move the mountain out of your way, that means He needs you to trust that He will give you the strength to climb it. We never get to a place of arrival. There's never a moment when you arrive and no longer have to do God's work.

There will never be a moment when devotion to Scripture isn't needed, when prayer no longer serves a purpose, when spending alone time with God isn't necessary. We must practice these disciplines daily until we are ushered into the presence of God and no longer have a physical body and mind to take care of. Whatever you're praying and asking for is merely a steppingstone to something greater. As the enemy continues to search for people to devour (see 1 Peter 5:8), God continues to equip us to handle it; therefore, you must always get back up and keep fighting the good fight.

My hope for you is that this book helps you have a better understanding of why prayer exists, what prayer truly means, and why it's not an obligation but a privilege. Prayer is not just a means to get by. Prayer is not a lifeless ritual or a set of words you recite out of constraint. Prayer is heartfelt, daily communication with the One who created you. It's something for which you should be longing. It is something that should fill and complete you. When you pray, you are connected to the Source of your life with an open line of communication. Being able to speak with God anytime you want is one of the greatest privileges you will ever receive. I pray that you don't take that lightly.

Your pain cannot stop His plan for you, so pray through your pain. Your fear cannot stop the purpose He has for you, so pray through your fear. Your doubt cannot stop Him from guiding you, so pray through your doubt. Your insecurities cannot stop His grace for you, so pray through your insecurities. Your shame cannot stop His mercy for you, so pray through your shame. Your anger cannot stop His sovereignty in your life, so pray through your anger. Your mistakes cannot stop His compassion for you, so pray through your mistakes.

There's nothing that can stop the transformational love of Jesus from operating in your life. It's always available—you only have to take hold of it.

THANK YOU PRAYER

Father God, I want to thank You regardless of what You give me. Your character isn't dependent upon my circumstances changing. You are holy! You are good! You are faithful! My trust and my faith are fully in You. Help me to see that no prayer that I pray goes unanswered. Help me to see the ways in which You respond, and give me the wisdom to know that You are for me and never against me. I'm going to shout Your praises in the middle of the storms, in the heat of the battle, and as I'm navigating through the tragedy and turmoil that comes with life. Thank You for never leaving me nor forsaking me and for always working things out for my good and for Your glory. Change my heart, change my point of view, and change the way that I respond when things don't go according to my plan. Lord, I love You. I pray this all in Jesus' mighty name, Amen.

APPLICATION

1. Share a time when God answered a prayer in a big way. How did you feel? How did it affect your prayer life? Did you share it with others?

2. Now reverse that thought. Share a time when you feel as if God didn't answer your prayer. How did you feel? How did it affect your prayer life? Did you share it with others?

3. With what you've learned about prayer in this book, identify the differences between how you respond to

getting what you want versus not getting what you asked for. How can you apply this to your prayer life? What things can you change to ensure that your view of God doesn't shift based on how He responds to your prayer requests?

Acknowledgments

My first acknowledgment is and always will be to God. All glory to Him for making this project come alive, allowing me to be a part of the process and trusting me as a vessel. This is His story, and it is an honor to be a small piece of the puzzle and to have the privilege of stewarding it. I pray that when people read this book, they understand this is all of Him and none of me.

I must thank my amazing wife, Kyra, who spent endless hours reviewing my early draft of this book, for giving me advice on the cover, and for brainstorming with me on the title. She was as essential to the completion of this book as I was. Thank you to my beautiful bride.

I am extremely grateful for all of those who I had the pleasure to work with in Chosen Books. They dedicated their time to making sure the vision God gave me for this book came to pass. Each member provided me extensive personal and professional guidance and showcased the love of God every step of the way.

Andrew F Carter is the founder and lead pastor of Royal City Church. His never-ending mission is to lead people to Jesus by spreading the Gospel around the world. Andrew travels as a guest speaker at churches, events, conferences, and retreats. He is known for his testimony of going from "Prisoner to Pastor," appearing on television networks, podcasts, and stages preaching the Good News of Jesus Christ and sharing his experience of our Father's transformational love. Andrew is an influencer, writer, husband, and father. Andrew and his wife, Kyra, live in Los Angeles, California. To learn more about Andrew, visit andrewfcarter.com. You can also find Andrew on all major social media platforms @andrewfcarter.